The Case of the Catalans

WHY SO MANY CATALANS NO LONGER WANT TO BE PART OF SPAIN

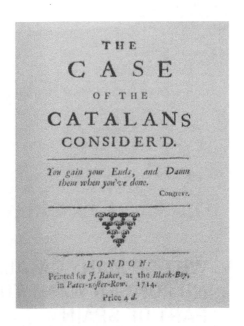

THE

CASE

OF THE

CATALANS

CONSIDER'D.

You gain your Ends, and Damn them when you've done.

Congreve.

LONDON:
Printed for *J. Baker*, at the *Black-Boy*, in *Pater-noster-Row*. 1714.
Price 4 d.

Title page of the book, published in 1714, which inspired the title of this book, *The Case of the Catalans* (2020).

The Case of the Catalans was the term used in the European chanceries in discussions regarding the political destiny of Catalonia in the context of the Peace of Utrecht (1712–1714) that ended the War of the Spanish Succession. After pledging support to the Catalans siding with the Habsburg pretender in the treaty of Genoa in 1705, England pulled out of the war in 1713 signing the Treaty of Utrecht, obtaining Gibraltar and Menorca, and access to the Spanish slave market. The abandoned Catalans continued fighting but were defeated by Bourbon troops after the dramatic siege of Barcelona in 1714.

The case was a matter of heated debates in the British Parliament and a number of books were published. *The Case of the Catalans consider'd* praised Catalan resistance in defence of their institutions and freedoms:

'Their Ancestors were given the privileges they enjoyed for centuries. Are they now to relinquish them without honour and leave behind them a race of slaves? No; They prefer to die all; Either death or freedom, this is their resolute choice'.

The Case of the Catalans

WHY SO MANY CATALANS NO LONGER WANT TO BE PART OF SPAIN

Edited by CLARA PONSATÍ
with contributions by
ANTONI ABAT NINET,
ENRIQUETA ARAGONÈS,
CARLES BOIX,
ALBERT CARRERAS,
XAVIER CUADRAS-MORATÓ
and
JORDI MUÑOZ

Luath Press Limited
EDINBURGH
www.luath.co.uk

First published 2020

ISBN: 978-1-913025-38-0

The paper used in this book is recyclable.
It is made from low chlorine pulps
produced in a low energy, low emissions
manner from renewable forests.

Printed and bound by
Ashford Colour Press, Gosport

Typeset in 11 point Din by Lapiz

Catalonia will return, peacefully and anxious to be a good neighbour, if she too is shown good neighbourliness; rough, distracted, and a source of permanent trouble, if she is tortured. For the sake of all nations, and especially of Spain, one may utter the fervent hope that Catalonia is witnessing the end of her tragic interlude.

Josep Trueta, *The Spirit of Catalonia* (1946)

Catalonia (highlighted) and Spain (Shutterstock)

The Principality of Catalonia (1608) (Public domain)

Contents

Timeline

From 878 – The Counts of Barcelona begin to distance themselves from the Carolingian Empire.

1137 – The Count of Barcelona marries the heir to the Aragonese Crown. It is the start of Catalonia's history within the Aragon Crown, but with a Catalan lineage ('Casa de Barcelona' – the House of Barcelona). The first mentions of the term Catalonia appear during this period.

1359 – The Generalitat de Catalunya is established, with a president and one of Europe earliest parliaments.

1410 – Martí l'Humà, the last king of the House of Barcelona, dies with no heir.

1412 – In the Casp compromise representatives of Aragon, Catalonia and Valencia meet to vote in a new royal house. They decide, by majority, to appoint Ferdinand of Antequera, a member of the Trastamara house, the family that holds the Castilian crown.

1469 – Ferdinand of Trastamara, heir of Aragon, marries Isabella, the heir of Castile. He becomes king of Aragon in 1479.

1474 – First printed book in Catalan appears.

1516-7 – Ferdinand is succeeded as King of Aragon by his grandson Charles, from the Habsburg dynasty.

1517–1700 – The Habsburg monarchs rule as kings of the separate Aragonese and Castilian Crowns. Within Aragon, they swear to separate Catalan constitutions.

1640 – Catalan Revolt against the Spanish monarchy.

1641 – Pau Claris, 94th President of the Generalitat, proclaims the brief Catalan Republic under the protection of France.

1650 – War ends when Spain and France sign the Treaty of the Pyrénées, in which Catalonia loses its northern territories.

1700 – Charles II, the last Habsburg king, dies without heirs. Philip V, grandson of Louis XIV of France, is crowned king.

1705 – War of the Spanish Succession, that pitched the Bourbon Kings of France and Spain against all of Europe's other major powers, supporting Archduke Charles, a Habsburg claimant to the Spanish throne. The Catalans side with Habsburg in defence of their traditional autonomy.

1713 – As Archduke Charles becomes Holy Roman Emperor, he loses much of his support. The British resolve to end the war and sign the Treaty of Utrecht that settles the new distribution of powers in Europe and the colonial world. Abandoned, Catalonia keeps fighting.

1714 – Barcelona falls to the Bourbons after a 14-month siege on 11 Sept – thereafter celebrated as Catalonia's National Day.

1716 – 'Nova Planta' decree issued. Catalonia loses its constitutions and is administered from Madrid and in Barcelona through Captain Generals. The Catalan language is suppressed. From then on, Catalonia is ruled as a Spanish region rather than a distinctive entity.

1808–14 – Following Napoleon's invasions of Spain, Catalonia is governed as a province of the French Empire between 1812 and 1814.

1810–27 – Spanish American Wars of Independence. Spain loses most of its colonial Empire as its colonies in Central and South America gain independence.

1868–73 – Spain seeks a new monarch, and invites King Amadeo, from the Italian Savoy dynasty, to take the throne. He rules Spain from 1871 to 1873.

1873 – The First Spanish Republic is proclaimed, but is overthrown by the army just a few months later in 1874.

1898 – Spain is defeated by the United States in the Spanish-American War. This results in Cuba gaining independence, and Puerto Rico, Guam and the Philippines being annexed by the United States.

1901 – Formation of the bourgeois Catalan Regionalist League, supporting autonomy, not independence.

1914 – Limited self-government returned to Catalonia under the leadership of Enric Prat de la Riba.

1923 – Miguel Primo de Rivera imposes a military dictatorship in Spain. Catalan self-government and language suppressed once again.

1931 – With the collapse of the Primo de Rivera dictatorship, the second Spanish Republic is proclaimed. In Barcelona, Francesc Macià briefly proclaims a Catalan Republic, but renounces it in order to lead the autonomous Catalan government.

1934 – Following the election of a right wing Spanish government new Catalan president, Lluís Companys, declares independence. However, this regime is suppressed by the army and Companys is jailed.

1936 – The left-wing Popular Front government elected in Spain. Catalan autonomy is restored.

1936–9 – The Spanish Civil War rages between the Nationalists and Republicans, supported by Catalonia. The Nationalists are victorious, allowing General Franco to establish a dictatorship.

1939–75 – Francisco Franco rules over Spain. Democracy, Catalan culture and autonomy are suppressed. The use of Catalan language is forbidden once again.

1969 – Francisco Franco appoints Bourbon Prince Juan Carlos his successor.

1975 – Francisco Franco dies and Juan Carlos I is declared King of Spain.

1976–7 – Adolfo Suárez is appointed Prime Minister and Spain begins its transition to democracy. In 1977 it holds its first democratic elections since the Second Republic.

1978 – Spain's new democratic constitution is approved by a referendum. Catalonia's autonomous institutions are restored.

1980 – Catalonia holds its first elections to the re-established Catalan Parliament. Jordi Pujol's CiU win and remain in power until 2003.

2003 – The CiU loses power to a left-wing coalition of the socialist PSC (led by Pasqual Maragall) the ERC and ICV.

2005–6 – A new Catalan Statute of Autonomy is passed through the Catalan Parliament in 2005, and approved by a referendum in Catalonia in 2006. The Spanish Constitutional Court begins deliberations on the new Statute. The Popular Party organises a Spain-wide campaign against any changes to the Constitution.

2010 – Spain's Constitutional Court rules the proposed new Catalan Statute of Autonomy unconstitutional. Large demonstrations against this decision are held in Barcelona. The CiU return to power in the Catalan government under the leadership of Artur Mas.

2012 – Catalan government makes plans for a 'consultation' on Catalan independence.

2014 – The Spanish Parliament and Constitutional Court both reject plans for an independence referendum. A consultative referendum is held regardless – drawing over 2.3 million votes, 1.9 of which support independence in the midst of a boycott by anti-independence groups.

2015 – The CiU and ERC form an alliance, 'Junts pel Sí', to contest a snap Catalan election, which they hope to use as a plebiscite on independence. This alliance, alongside other pro-independence groups, gains 47.8 per cent of the vote and an absolute majority of seats in the Catalan Parliament. The new government declares that start of a 'process' towards independence.

2016 – Artur Mas steps down as President of the Catalan Generalitat in favour of Carles Puigdemont, with the support of Junts pel Sí and the far-left CUP.

2017 – Catalan referendum on independence held. 2.3 million votes are cast out of a total electoral roll of 5.3 million – anti-independence groups again boycotted the vote, with 2 million favouring independence. The Catalan Parliament declares independence. The Spanish government suspends the Catalan government and either arrests or forces into exile a number of pro-independence leaders. New Catalan elections are called, yet pro-independence groups secure another majority.

2018 – Three attempts to elect a new Catalan President fail over the course of several months as the candidates are either in exile or prison. Joaquim Torra is eventually elected as Catalan President and a new government formed. PP loses motion of no confidence and PSOE takes Spanish government.

2019 – The Spanish Supreme Court declares that nine former Catalan leaders are guilty of sedition and sentences them to 9 to 13 years in prison. The verdict sparks massive protests throughout the country, blocking Barcelona's airport and main streets.

List of abbreviations and glossary

ANC: **Assemblea Nacional Catalana** (Catalan National Assembly). Grassroots civic association that seeks the political independence of Catalonia. Famous for holding mass demonstrations. Formed officially in March 2012, Carme Forcadell was its first President and was succeeded by Jordi Sànchez. Both are now in prison.

AN: **Audiencia Nacional** (National Audience). A special Spanish penal court with no territorial ground established for cases of particular 'national interest'. It was established in January 1977 to replace the Tribunal de Orden Público, Franco's special court that prosecuted political dissidents under the dictatorship.

Catalunya en Comú-Podem (Catalonia in Common-We Can!). Left-wing electoral coalition comprising Podem, the Catalan Branch of Podemos, and Catalunya en Comú, a local grouping organised by Barcelona mayor Ada Colau. It includes Iniciativa per Catalunya-Verds (ICV), the successor to the Catalan communist PSUC. Between 2015 and 2017, they ran under the name Catalunya Sí Que Es Pot (CSQEP).

CEO: **Centre d'Estudis d'Opinió** (Centre for Opinion Studies). Survey opinion polls office run by the Catalan Government.

CIS: **Centro de Investigacions Sociológicas** (Centre for Sociological Research). Survey opinion polls office run by the Spanish Government.

Congreso de los Diputados (Spanish Congress). Spanish legislative chamber. It has 350 members elected by 50 provincial constituencies by proportional representation using the D'Hondt method.

CSA: **Estatut d'Autonomia de Catalunya** (Catalan Statute of Autonomy). Charter regulating Catalan self-government within Spain. A first statute was approved under the Second Spanish Republic in 1932. After the Generalitat was re-established in 1977, a CSA was introduced under the Spanish Constitution of 1978. A reform of the CSA was approved by the Catalan Parliament and passed through the Spanish Congress subject to amendments, in 2006. This reformed CSA was challenged in the Constitutional Court by the PP, among others. The landmark 2010 decision by the Constitutional Court that dismissed the reformed CSA is considered the trigger of the present crisis.

Tribunal Constitucional (Constitutional Court). The arbitral body that interprets the Spanish constitution to resolve constitutional disputes, and as chamber of last appeal above the Supreme Court in cases related to fundamental rights.

Consejo General del Poder Judicial (General Council of the Judiciary). The collegiate government of Spain's judges. It appoints magistrates and prosecutors at the Supreme Court, the regional high courts, and the Audiencia Nacional, and makes all other kinds of decisions that determine the career path of judges, from post allocations, to promotions, sanctions, or suspensions.

CIU: **Convergència i Unió** (Convergence and Union). Catalanist centre-right electoral alliance comprising Democratic Convergence of Catalonia and the smaller Democratic Union of Catalonia. Founded in 1978, it dissolved in 2015 upon disagreements on whether to take a pro-independence stance. Under Jordi Pujol, CIU ran the autonomous Catalan government for 23 years between 1980 and 2003. It sought to secure the greatest possible devolution of powers within Spain, rather than independence. It returned to power in 2010 under Artur Mas and took on increasingly pro-independence positions until the coalition broke.

C's: Ciudadanos (Citizens' Party). Spanish neo-liberal, anti-independence party launched in Catalonia in 2006 and later extended to the rest of Spain.

Ciutadans (Citizens' Party). Catalan branch of Ciudadanos.

Convergència Democratica de Catalunya (Democratic Convergence of Catalonia). Leading Catalan autonomist party later renamed PDeCat. The largest constituent of the old CIU coalition. Its leaders included Jordi Pujol and Artur Mas.

CUP: **Candidatures d'Unitat Popular** (Popular Unity Candidacies). Far-left political organisation in Catalonia that favours independence from Spain. Traditionally focused on municipal politics and organised around local assemblies.

ERC: **Esquerra Republicana de Catalunya** (Republican Left of Catalonia). Catalan party founded in 1931 by the union of Estat Catalan (Catalan State) led by

Francesc Macià and the Catalan Republican Party of Lluís Companys.

Generalitat de Catalunya (Catalan Regional Government). Name traditionally given to the Catalan government.

Guardia Civil (Civil Guard). Spanish state para-military security force founded in 1844. It maintains military discipline and draws officers from the army.

ICV: **Iniciativa per Catalunya Verds** (Initiative for Catalonia Greens). Merger of the PSUC, the former Catalan communists, and Green Party.

Junts per Catalunya (Together for Catalonia). Electoral front created by Carles Puigdemont's PDeCAT to run in the December 2017 Catalan election. It included independent figures such as Jordi Sánchez, the jailed leader of the ANC.

Junts pel Sí (Together for Yes). Electoral coalition formed by pro-independence parties to run in the 2015 Catalan election, led by Artur Mas. Included PDeCAT, ERC and independents.

Òmniun Cultural. A civic association that promotes and defends the Catalan language and culture. Established in 1961 under the Franco regime when the public and institutional use of Catalan was illegal. Played a key role since 2012 in organising pro-independence demonstrations. Òmniun President, Jordi Cuixart, has been in prison since October 2017.

Parlament de Catalunya (Catalan Parliament). Catalan legislature.

PDeCAT: **Partit Demòcrata Europeu Català** (Catalan European Democratic Party). Catalan party founded in

2016 by Artur Mas. Direct successor of the now-defunct Democratic Convergence of Catalonia. Under Artur Mas and his successor Carles Puigdemont, it has broken with the traditionally autonomist position of its predecessor party and now openly supports independence.

PNV: **Partido Nacionalista Vasco** (Basque Nationalist Party). In Basque: Euzko Alderdi Jeltzalea (EAJ). Traditional, conservative Basque nationalist party founded in 1895.

Podemos (We Can!). Spanish far-left party founded in 2014 in the aftermath of the 15 May anti-austerity protests. It has been led by Pablo Iglesias since its creation.

PP: **Partido Popular** (People's Party). Dominant party of the post-Franco Spanish right founded in 1989. In government in Spain from 1996 until 2004 under José María Aznar. It returned to power in December 2011 under Mariano Rajoy who was the Spanish President during the October 2017 crisis. He was removed from power by a motion of no-confidence in 2018.

PSC: **Partit dels Socialistes de Catalunya** (Socialist Party of Catalonia). Catalan branch of the main Spanish Socialist Party, the PSOE, in the post-Franco era. The PSC governed Catalonia in coalition with ERC and ICV from 2003 to 2010.

PSOE: **Partido Socialista Obrero Español** (Spanish Socialist Workers' Party). Main Spanish centre-left socialist party, founded in 1879. Formed post-Franco governments under Felipe González between 1982 and 1996 and José Luis Rodríguez-Zapatero from 2004 until 2011. It returned to power in July 2018 under Pedro Sánchez.

Senado (Spanish Senate). The upper chamber of Spain's Parliament. It is made up of 266 members: 208 elected by popular vote, and 58 appointed by the regional legislatures.

Spanish Constitution. The Constitution was drafted, debated and approved by the legislature that emerged from the 1977 general election, and approved in a national referendum in 1978.

Tribunal Supremo (Supreme Court). The highest court in Spain for all matters not pertaining to the Spanish Constitution.

UCD: **Unión de Centro Democrático** (Centre Democratic Union). Party set up by Spanish President Adolfo Suárez, a conglomerate of former Francoist reformers that led Spain's transition to democracy. UCD won Spain's first democratic election in 1977 and remained in power until 1982, when they were severely defeated by the PSOE. The party subsequently disintegrated.

Introduction

Why are so many Catalans no longer happy to be a part of Spain? This book reviews the historical, legal, political and economic aspects of the present conflict between Catalonia and Spain and seeks to provide answers to this question.

Catalonia is a small territory in the north – east corner of the Iberian Peninsula in southern Europe, home to 7.8 million people. This land of 32,000 square km makes up just 6.3 per cent of Spain's territory, similar in size to Belgium, yet contains 16.2 per cent of its population. Its capital is the world-renowned city of Barcelona. Catalonia is a relatively rich region. It contributes to 20.1 per cent Spain's total GDP, and its per capita GDP is higher than both the Spanish and EU average by 19.9 and 10.2 per cent respectively. Catalonia is the export powerhouse of Spain – over one quarter of Spanish exports are produced in Catalonia – and it is a major tourist destination. Despite this great potential for prosperity, the country's structurally high unemployment rates, 11.5 per cent compared to 20.4 per cent in 2020, are a major constraint on its competitiveness and social cohesion.

Catalans are an old European people with their own language, a long and distinct history, and a strong sense of national identity. Yet, Catalonia is a nation without a particular ethnic component. From its medieval origins to the present day, Catalonia has always been a 'land of through travel', welcoming and assimilating a diversity of peoples and individuals. Catalan identity has been constructed on resistance against being assimilated by a hostile state. Present day Catalans are a complex and very diverse bunch. Since the beginning of the 20th century, Catalonia has experienced three important waves of immigration. The first two, between 1901 to 1930 and 1951 to 1975, brought people from the rest of Spain. The proportion of residents in Catalonia born elsewhere in Spain peaked in 1970 at 36.6 per cent. The third and most recent wave started in 2000 and ended abruptly with the start of the economic crisis in 2009. It was nonetheless very substantial, pushing population growth to 17.6 per cent in seven years, more than three times the 5.1 per cent growth of the period between 1981 and 2000. More importantly, migrants were not just arriving from other parts of Spain, but from the rest of the world, mostly from African and Latin American countries, as well as Europe. As a consequence of these strong immigration flows, the percentage of the population residing in Catalonia who were not born in Spain rose from 6.1 per cent in 2001 to 18.2 per cent in 2018. Undoubtedly, immigration is a crucial feature in the configuration of Catalan society that has major linguistic, social, and political implications.

Since the Industrial Revolution, Catalonia has been Spain's main economic engine and a key agent in its modernisation. Throughout their tumultuous 19th and 20th century histories, Catalans have always longed for self-government. Yet, the dream of an independent Catalan Republic has repeatedly been confronted by strident Spanish imperial nationalism. After 40 years of harsh dictatorship and Spanish chauvinism under Franco, the constitution approved in 1978 established the legal and political basis for a regime of regional self-government whereby Catalonia was one among 17 autonomous regions throughout the whole of Spain. To the majority of Catalans, this seemed a good starting point for ensuring self-government and material progress. Opinion surveys and electoral contests consistently indicated that only a politically insignificant minority preferred independence at this point.

However, in 2010, to the surprise of many qualified observers of the international political scene, popular support for independence surged. Massive peaceful demonstrations organised by civil society in support of independence took to the streets on 11 September (the Catalan National Day) year after year from 2012 to 2019. Following the regional elections of November 2012, the Catalan Parliament and Regional Government made several unsuccessful attempts to gain the agreement of Spanish institutions for a referendum on Catalonia's status within Spain. In 2017, continuous disagreement resulted in the Catalan Government's unilateral organisation of a self-determination referendum on 1 October and then a declaration of independence on 27 October. The Spanish authorities responded to this with the suspension of regional self-governing institutions and the incarceration or exile of pro-independence political leaders.

Why would Catalans want to be independent? The simple answer might be because Catalonia is a nation and all peoples have the right to freedom and self-determination. But in the 21st century, in the European Union, the present Catalan conflict is not a classic nationalist emancipation process. Why would Catalans want to engage in an uphill fight to set up an independent state in 21st century

Europe? The answer is collective frustration and democratic determination. Over the years it has become evident that the Spanish constitutional system established in 1978 had not only stopped evolving in the direction of assuring Catalan self-government, but had clearly regressed to work against Catalan interests. Furthermore, as the Catalans' demands for self-determination advanced and the response of Spanish institutions grew increasingly authoritarian, such demands could only be reinforced. The inability of Spanish institutions and politicians to manage the crisis with respect for fundamental rights and freedom of expression has seriously undermined the quality of democracy in Spain.

How did we get here? In what follows, we examine this question from a variety of points of view to uncover the reasons that feed the present struggle for Catalan independence. This book is a collective work combining contributions by seven Catalan academics. The text is composed of 6 chapters, each a stand-alone essay, that can be read independently or concurrently with the others. Each of us initially drafted materials for one or two of the chapters, and we subsequently worked together to produce the final text.

Chapter 1 (written by Clara Ponsatí) contextualises the main issues contention in the political controversy. We examine the main arguments of the political disagreement, paying close attention to the conditions under which the Spanish constitution of 1978 was drafted and approved, and how these initial conditions have shaped the evolution of Spanish democracy and its institutions. We pay particular attention to the major dysfunctions in the judiciary and in the constitutional court that have undermined democratic checks and balances up to the present point of collapse.

Chapter 2 (written by Albert Carreras) provides a long-run historical background with an overview of Catalan history from its medieval origins up to the approval of the Catalan Statute of Autonomy in 1979 under the Spanish Constitution. It examines the formation of a distinct Catalan political identity and two conflicts with Castile – in particular the 1640 Secession war and the early 18th century Succession war that put an end to Catalan constitutions and self-government. After Catalonia's full absorption into Spain, these conflicts did not disappear, even if, for a few generations, it seemed that Catalonia and the Catalans had become accepted as Spanish. Most of the text focuses on the century before 1979, covering the rise of modern Catalanism as a reaction to Spanish attempts to fully dissolve Catalan identity, leading to what appeared in 1979 to be a lasting success after various failed attempts to achieve self-government.

Chapter 3 (written by Antoni Abat Ninet and Carles Boix) reviews the constitutional dispute. The decision of the Spanish Constitutional Court in June 2010 on the statute of autonomy of Catalonia has been widely considered as the trigger of the current conflict. However, the disagreement was long-standing, originating from the foundation of the constitution. Spain has unsuccesfully attempted to reconcile its political organisation with the national aspirations of the Basque, Catalan and Galician peoples. We examine how the constitution addressed the framing of territorial tensions, how the evolution of such a territorial model led to the reform of the Statute of Autonomy of 2006, and we explain the decision of the Constitutional Court that dismissed this attempt at reform.

Chapter 4 (written by Enriqueta Aragonès and Jordi Muñoz) analyses how and why independence has become the central issue of Catalan politics. Between 2010 and 2013,

Catalonia witnessed a rapid and intense realignment of political preferences, leading to almost half of the electorate coming to support independence. Positions have hardened, and both the pro- and anti-independence camps have become increasingly entrenched and intensely mobilised. We describe the importance of civil society and grassroots organisations in the rise of the pro-independence movement, and how they have forced Catalan political parties to revise their electoral platforms. We also analyse the negotiations and disagreements between the Catalan and the Spanish governments and their impact on electoral politics. The failure to reach an agreement, and the realignment of political parties' polarised agendas over Catalan independence, have precipitated the present crisis.

Chapter 5 (written by Xavier Cuadras-Morató) looks at the economic costs and benefits of Catalan independence. We identify and analyse the main opportunities for and threats to the Catalan economy in an independent state, as well as in a potential future transition period to the new status of an independent state. Catalonia, as a relatively modern and prosperous European state, would enjoy better opportunities from greater political power, especially relating to fiscal resources and independent public policies, although it could suffer from the potential reduction in economic interaction with what remained of Spain – currently its main economic partner. The transition process to independence, which has involved a very serious political conflict, has so far had a small economic impact, but if the current deadlock persists, it could affect the prospects of the country in a more serious way.

Chapter 6 (written by Carles Boix) tackles the right of Catalans to self-determination. We review the evolution of the principle of self-determination in international law. We first illustrate that it has been explicitly formalised for territories under colonial administration. Secondly, we highlight that even in other contexts in which it is not explicitly formalised, the principle of self-determination has been deemed permissible provided that those that exercise it comply with two key conditions. These are the principle *uti possidetis* (i.e. that newly-formed sovereign states should retain the internal borders that their preceding dependent area had before their independence) and the absence of illicit violence. Moving beyond the legality of the right of self-determination, the chapter proceeds to summarise the main normative justifications that the current jurisprudence and philosophical debates require to legitimise the use of the principle of self-determination, connecting them to the Catalan crisis. The chapter concludes by discussing why the Catalan case may be treated as an instance of 'internal enlargement' within the European Union.

The publication of this book was intended for early 2020 but the outbreak of the coronavirus pandemic has delayed it for several months. This means that our review does not include the latest developments. Nevertheless, the past few months have not brought any significant development towards the resolution of the Catalan conflict: if anything, the new Spanish government's management of the COVID pandemic and its failure to carry out any steps towards a negotiated solution have only deepened the conflict. Therefore, the question the book sets to answer –'Why are so many Catalans no longer happy to be a part of Spain?'– and the answers we try to provide remains just as relevant for understanding the current Catalan crisis.

Spanish democracy meets its limits

1 In September of 2017, following the elected mandate of the majority in the Catalan Parliament, the Government of Catalonia called for a referendum on independence to take place on 1 October. Within hours, the Spanish Constitutional Court declared the referendum unconstitutional. On the eve of referendum day, thousands of anti-riot Spanish police were brought from outside Catalonia to prevent it. On 1 October, they were unleashed with orders to harshly attack voters in what has been recorded as one of the worst episodes of violence against peaceful civilians in Western Europe since 1945. Yet, in spite of police violence, over 2.3 million citizens voted, and 90 per cent of them cast ballots in favour of independence. In the chaotic days that followed, the Catalan Parliament declared independence, and then the Spanish Senate suspended the Catalan Parliament and sacked the regional government. Criminal charges were brought against the Speaker of the Catalan Parliament, the Catalan Government and two leaders of the grassroots organisations Assemblea Nacional Catalana and Òmnium Cultural. The Catalan President Carles Puigdemont and four other members of his government went into exile. Courts have since opened criminal cases against over 900 citizens, political party and grassroots leaders, mayors, senior public officials, teachers, police officers, firemen, entrepreneurs, web makers, singers and others.

After the suspension of the Catalan Government and Parliament in November 2017, an election to the Catalan Parliament was held on 21 December and resulted in the return of another pro-independence majority. However, Spanish authorities refused to accept this result. Catalonia remained for months under the control of the Spanish government of the PP (a party that held just four out of 135 seats in the Catalan Parliament), and several potential candidates to take lead of the Catalan government were vetoed by the Spanish Supreme court. One of them, Jordi Turull, was taken back to prison the day after defending his candidacy. Eventually, the pro-independence majority agreed to appoint an 'acceptable' candidate in the form of Joaquim Torra in mid-May 2018.

Shortly later, the verdict for the Gürtel case – one of many ongoing trials for alleged corruption affecting the PP – was announced. The ruling established that the Prime Minister's party had profited from an illegal 'kickbacks-for-contracts' scheme. This prompted a vote of no-confidence against Prime Minister Mariano Rajoy in the Spanish Congress. Rajoy was dismissed and the PSOE's leader Pedro Sánchez appointed with the aid of the Catalan parties' votes. There was an expectation that the confrontation might ease and some form of political dialogue with the Catalan government could begin. But those hopes proved unfounded. The criminal case against government members and civic leaders was on trial at the Spanish Supreme Court in the spring of 2019, and the verdict was announced on 14 October 2019. Nine of the defendants were declared guilty of sedition and sentenced to harsh prison terms ranging from nine to 13 years.

After a few months in office, the Sánchez minority government failed to approve its budget and a snap election took place on 28 April. In Catalonia, the number of pro-independence MPs increased from 17 to 22, with the ERC claiming first place across Catalonia. Sánchez claimed victory, with the PSOE substantially increasing its vote. Yet his party fell short of an absolute majority. Pro-independence forces maintained their strength in the Municipal and European Parliament elections that followed shortly on 25 May. Exiles Puigdemont and former minister Antoni Comín and one of the political prisoners, former vice-president Oriol Junqueras leader of the ERC, were elected as MEPs. However, Spain refused to acknowledge them as MEPs. When the European Parliament reconvened in Strasbourg on 2 July 2019, they were not allowed to take their seats, and Junqueras remained imprisoned.

During the summer of 2019, Sanchez attempted to obtain majority support to become Prime Minister, but he failed. Hence a new election was held 10 November. While Sánchez's PSOE came out on top again, with a small loss of three seats, the results again delivered a blocked Congress, with a coalition to end the government's long deadlock ever more difficult. The far right Francoist nostalgic VOX party doubled its vote share to take third position, and Ciudadanos was almost wiped out falling to ten seats from 57. Catalan pro-independence MPs increased their vote share and gained one seat. This time, Sánchez agreed to a coalition government with Podemos. With the support of Basque nationalist and other small parties, and with the crucial abstention of Junqueras' ERC, he managed a slim majority to be confirmed as Prime Minister on 7 January. Whether the Sánchez coalition government will take steps to resolve the Catalan conflict is still too early to tell.

The European and international outlook of the conflict is making headway as Spain's reiterated attempts to arrest Puigdemont and his ministers in exile fail as they meet with independent judicial scrutiny at Belgian, German and Scottish courts. The first round of European arrest warrants were withdrawn on 4 December 2017 by Supreme Court justice Pablo Llerena after the Belgian court that examined them had already heard the case and was about to deliver a decision. In the second round, the case against Puigdemont was examined in Germany where he had been arrested in March 2018. The charges of rebellion and sedition were conclusively dismissed. Not willing to accept an extradition on minor charges, Llerena again withdrew the warrants. He issued a third round of arrest warrants in October 2019 as a follow up the Supreme Court verdict. At the time of writing, these are still open before courts in Belgium and Scotland (for Clara Ponsatí) and promise to be quite complex to resolve as the case now affects elected MEPs. Indeed, after the European Parliament election, this judicial saga has escalated into an open conflict between the Spanish Supreme court and the European Court of Justice. Because Junqueras remained in prison in spite of being an elected MEP, and Puigdemont and Comín were not allowed to take their seats either, their cases were taken to the European Court of Justice. On 19 December 2019, the European court ruled against Spain: the elected MEPs were to take their seats, they were entitled to parliamentary immunity, and consequently Junqueras should be freed. Puigdemont and Comín where recognised as MEPs, but the Spanish Supreme Court refused to let Junqueras free and so entered into an open conflict with the European Court of Justice.

This major political crisis has de facto terminated the constitutional covenant of 1978, the founding stone of today's Spanish democracy. The Spanish majority bloc frames this constitutional conflict in terms of Catalan lack of respect for the 'rules of the game' set by the constitution of 1978. According to this discourse, there is a unique, indivisible Spanish nation that is the sole subject of sovereignty, meaning that the recognition of other sources of sovereignty (i.e. the Catalan nation) is impossible. The constraints imposed by this interpretation of the constitution are so tight that they rule out any negotiation for a political solution. First, as long as the majority controls the rules of the game without restraint, no change to those rules seems achievable. Second, without recognising the minority as a political actor, the only solution Spain is capable of accepting is the surrender of the minority. Understanding the situation in Catalonia requires critical scrutiny of this 'constitutional' narrative. And to that end, we must recall the conditions under which the constitution was drafted and approved in 1978, and keep in mind how these initially authoritarian conditions have shaped the evolution of Spanish democracy. Further to this, observers must be aware of the poor democratic health of the Spanish judicial system and of the unusual role of the Constitutional Court to understand the reasons why the checks and balances indispensable for any democracy have collapsed. We will discuss each of these in turn next.

The genesis and legitimacy of the 1978 Constitution

The conditions under which Spain became a formal Western-style democracy and the Spanish constitution was approved are not widely known. In fact, the political situation in Spain after Franco's death in 1975 was so complex, and the danger of the country falling into chaos so obvious, that it was considered an unqualified success that firstly, some form of democracy was provided by the constitution approved in 1978; and, secondly, that it could be developed and implemented in the following years. However, the authoritarian context in which that constitution was drawn up and then voted on must be remembered and highlighted as a part of the explanation of why Spain and Catalonia are now stuck in a major political crisis.

Political theorists and constitutional law experts generally agree that constitutions must be drawn from an assembly with an explicit mandate to do so. People must know they are voting to elect representatives whose function it is to draw a constitution. This is crucial to ensure fairness. This was not the case for the Spanish assembly elected in June 1977. Furthermore, important political parties were not authorised to run in the election (among them the ERC, a major player in the current Catalan Parliament, which was still illegal). While the constitution was being discussed, violence, including deaths and bombings, was a regular feature in the streets. According to French historian Sophie Baby, 714 people met politically motivated violent deaths in the period from 1975 to 1982, 178 of whom were direct victims of police violence. The Army had a prominent political role, its top officers were still Franco's appointees and the laws that entitled them to intervene in political life remained in force. All the police forces, including its top commanders, were those of the Franco regime. The dictatorship had been a one-party political system. The only legal party, Franco's fascist organisation, had its own propaganda apparatus, including radio stations and newspapers in the most important provincial towns.

Public radio stations and the two public TV channels – there were no private channels at the time – were under tight governmental control. These were the conditions under which the constitution of 1978 was drafted, discussed and voted.

Furthermore, as is now publicly acknowledged by surviving members of the committee who drafted the constitution, several crucial articles were 'dictated from above', i.e. by the Crown and the Army. Their wording was literally incorporated into the final text of the constitution as ordered. These were the fundamental articles that concerned key elements of the political structure of the state. The most prominent ones were: 1) Spain had to be a monarchy; 2) The only sovereignty was that of the Spanish nation; Catalonia and the Basque Country had to be explicitly subordinated to the one and only nation, Spain; 3) The military were ultimately responsible with preserving the unity of Spain. Hence, the authoritarian conditions that in 1977 and 1978 shaped and curtailed the writing and approval of the Spanish constitution to a large extent invalidate the constitution's legitimacy as a democratic framework. It is a constitution whose limits were drawn by an authoritarian regime.

Before setting out to draft the constitution, in October 1977 the Spanish Congress had passed the Law of Amnesty. The law freed political prisoners and permitted those exiled to return to Spain, but at the same time it guaranteed impunity for those who participated in the crimes of the Franco regime. This law institutionalised a pact of forgetfulness and equated victims and perpetrators. It is still in force, and has prevented any investigation into the crimes of the Franco regime, which amounted to a 'Spanish Holocaust' – as has been well-documented by historian Paul Preston. At least 114,226 'disappeared' remain to be uncovered in around 2,500 mass graves that have yet to be excavated. Approximately 400,000 political prisoners were used as forced labourers, but businesses that employed them have not been held accountable. Thousands of people who suffered torture, ill-treatment and detention, and victims 'executed' by Franco during the Civil War and the first years of repression, continue to appear as criminals in the records of Spanish justice. The list of victims is endless. However, thanks to the Law of Amnesty, the Francoist elite was granted impunity for crimes. After 1978, former ministers of Franco remained powerful and thrived in politics and business; judges, military and police officers kept their jobs. The servants of the criminal regime remained entrenched in the state apparatus, crucially shaping its development under the new conditions. While the Republican dead are still in the ditches and their families continue waiting for truth, justice and reparation, just as they have since 1939, Francoist impunity pervades Spain's political culture.

Beyond its origins, the application and deployment of any constitutional text depends, ultimately, on the structure of power and the decision mechanisms that are described within it. They depend, in other words, on who has been defined as the arbitrators for the interpretation of the constitutional text. Thus, the composition and evolution of legislatures, high courts and other institutions play a determining role in the evolution of the constitutional covenant. In the case of the Spanish constitution of 1978, the combination of a biased system of territorial representation, alongside the non-neutrality of the judiciary, were problematic from the start and have shaped the institutional evolution of Spain since 1977.

1

A constitution for the national majority

The system of territorial representation was a crucial component in the institutionalisation of democracy during the transition. It set the initial conditions which were decisive in the composition of the founding legislatures, and it has remained unchanged since then. The system, over-representing rural provinces, was explicitly designed by the Suárez government to assure the electoral victory of the post-Francoists in 1977. Provinces were taken as the constituency unit. Each province elects a minimum of two representatives to the Congress of Deputies, so that the small provincial constituencies are over-represented. Today, for example, each deputy elected for Soria represents about 45,000 people. In Madrid, each deputy represents about 180,000. The 40 smallest out of the 52 provinces represent approximately 40 per cent of the Spanish population, but they control over 50 per cent of the seats in the Congress of Deputies. Spain has the third most distorted representation in its lower house across Europe. Worldwide, its lower house is the 16th most distorted. In the Senate, where each province elects four senators, the difference is even more dramatic. Twenty per cent of the Spanish population elects half of the senators chosen by direct election.

Over-representation of under-populated provinces ensured a politically privileged position for the national parties that are especially strong in the small electoral districts. Consequently, it gives them the control of the majorities that appoint the members of the arbitral institutions like the Constitutional Court and the General Council of the

Judiciary. In this system, Catalonia does not have the capacity, due to its population and even less due to its political underrepresentation, to block any legislation. Such veto power would not be possible even if it were possible to construct an unlikely coalition with all the periphery territories including Valencia, the Balearic Islands, the Basque Country and Galicia.

The undemocratic roots of Spain's judicial system

The Francoist judicial system was never adequately reformed. The top justices of the dictatorship were chosen through their loyalty to the regime, and it was difficult to hold a judicial post without a 'clean' political background. Most of them, including those in charge of political repression, stayed active as justices under the new constitutional system after 1978.

Not even the notoriously cruel Tribunal de Orden Público, the special court that prosecuted political dissidents, was dissolved. Formally, the Tribunal de Orden Público ceased operations by Royal Decree in January 1977, two years after Franco's death. In its place, on the same day, in the very same building and with the same membership, the current Audiencia Nacional was established as a special court for cases of particular 'national interest'. Out of the 16 justices that made up the Tribunal de Orden Público in 1977, 10 ended up on the Audiencia Nacional or the Supreme Court of the new constitutional state. It is important to note that this occurred five months before the first elections, and almost two years before the approval of the constitution. Thus, the Audiencia Nacional is not a product of democracy.

The General Council of the Judiciary – the collegiate government of the judges – appoints magistrates and prosecutors at the Supreme Court, the regional high courts, and the Audiencia Nacional. Membership of this council needs confirmation by Congress with a 60 per cent majority approval; the result is a notoriously politically controlled organisation. In addition to appointments, the council makes all other kinds of decisions that determine the career path of judges, from post allocations to promotions, sanctions and suspensions. The GRECO, the Group of States against Corruption at the Council of Europe, has issued recurrent reports assessing the poor performance of Spain's judiciary, demanding legislative reform with regard to the appointment of prosecutors and judges, and emphasising the need for an 'evaluation of the legislative governing of the General Council of the Judiciary and its effect on the real and perceived independence of this body from any undue influence, with a view to remedying any shortcomings identified'. However, GRECO's last report in January 2018 concludes that none of its 11 recommendations contained in the previous reports has been implemented satisfactorily.[1]

The role of the Audiencia Nacional deserves further comment. A special penal court without territorial basis with the capacity to initiate criminal proceedings is an odd judicial scheme. Its existence is unique in Western Europe. The Audiencia Nacional has mostly focused on trials related to terrorism, international financial crimes and drug trafficking, but it has also spearheaded the persecution of pro-independence activists and politicians, first in the Basque Country and more recently in Catalonia. Audiencia Nacional justices routinely overstretch the definition of terrorism and are notorious for failing to investigate allegations against the Spanish state of torture and other human rights abuses. Even though the European Court of Human Rights has reversed decisions of the Audiencia in a number of cases, its justices have remained in their posts.

The example of magistrate Carmen Lamela – the judge that ordered the imprisonment of the Catalan leaders in October 2017 – provides a vivid illustration of how questionable use of judicial power not only goes unchecked, but also leads to reward. Lamela is responsible for the high profile case of Sandro Rosell, the former President of Barcelona F.C., who spent almost two years in pre-trial detention and was eventually acquitted of all charges. She was also responsible for the Altsasu case, where nine Basque youths where charged with terrorism for allegedly participating in a bar brawl with members of the Civil Guard. The youths spent a year and a half in pre-trial detention and were eventually sentenced for up to 13 years. Lamela also saw terrorism in the activities of the anarchist and vegan group Straight Edge in Madrid. Two activists spent more than one year imprisoned under a severe regime and were later acquitted. The judge also investigated 13 rappers of The Insurgency accused of terrorism, incitement to hatred, crime against state institutions, insults to the crown and unlawful association, for which the rappers were sentenced to two years and one day in prison. Lamela's harsh approach with Basques and Catalans is in contrast with her dealing of the case against construction tycoon and President of Real Madrid F.C. Florentino Pérez and five former Spanish ministers accused of prevarication, fraud and embezzlement after the failed construction of the Castor Project platform in the Mediterranean. The platform had started operating despite numerous technical reports advising against it, and was dismantled after causing a series of seismic events in the region. Nonetheless, the government compensated the contractor with €1,350 million. Judge Lamela swiftly dismissed all accusations. Lamela's notable 'service' has been handsomely rewarded. In July 2018, Carmen Lamela was promoted to the highest level of the Spanish judiciary and became a member of the Supreme Court. She may have been by far the weakest in the field of candidates, but this was no obstacle as she counted on powerful supporters including Carlos Lesmes, the president of the the Supreme Court and the General Council of the Judiciary, and Manuel Marchena, the magistrate presiding in the trial against the Catalan leaders.

On the Constitutional Court

Because the Francoist judiciary system, including the Supreme Court, remained practically untouched during the transition, and because the senior members of the judiciary had been educated in the legal dogmas of the Franco's regime, a Constitutional Court separate from the judiciary was established, as is also the case in the German and Italian constitutions. It was supposed to be an arbitral body, to resolve constitutional disputes, and a chamber of last appeal above the Supreme Court in cases related to fundamental rights. Members of the Constitutional Court are not required to be members of the judiciary; they can be judges, other esteemed academics or members of the law professional community. They are selected as follows: four are appointed by a 60 per cent majority vote of the Spanish Congress, four are appointed by a 60 per cent majority vote of the Senate, two are appointed by a 60 per cent majority vote of the General Council of the Judiciary, and two are appointed by the Spanish government. Regional autonomous governments or parliaments have no deciding voice or veto power on the composition of the Constitutional Court or the General Council of the Judiciary.

Initially, the Constitutional Court was composed mostly of distinguished individuals, and the Court was reasonably independent and immune to political pressure. However, over time, this has not proved sustainable. The two main political parties have actively used their control of the necessary 60 per cent majorities. They routinely reach horse-trading agreements to split the appointment of magistrates, and do so without regard to quality standards, and with no concern for appearances. The Constitutional Court has evolved into a highly partisan body, each member owing allegiance either to the Socialists or to the Popular Party, and all alienated from the Catalan minority. Under these circumstances, and especially after the Constitutional Court ruling dismissing the Catalan statute in 2010, the Constitutional Court effectively renounced its right to act as a neutral constitutional referee and lost its legitimacy.

Another illustrative example will help the reader to envision what kind of people Spanish political parties select to fill such high offices. Francisco Pérez de los Cobos was a member of the Constitutional Court from 2011 until 2017, and acted as its President between 2013 and 2017. Judge Pérez de los Cobos was a member of the Popular Party, but he did not report this fact prior to his appointment. When this information was disclosed, he did not resign nor was he removed. He was recently proposed by Spain for the ECHR, but his candidacy was turned down after he had submitted a CV claiming proficiency in English and French yet could not answer the questions of the appointments committee in either of those languages. As President of the Court, Pérez de los Cobos issued the ruling declaring the Catalan referendum illegal. In 1978, together with his family, he had actively campaigned against the approval of the constitution. Pérez de los Cobos comes from old pro-Franco stock and is well connected. His father had run as a candidate for the ultra-Francoist Fuerza Nueva, a party aiming to 'keep alive the ideals of 18 July 1936' in the 1977 Spanish general election. His brother, Diego Pérez de los Cobos, is a Colonel of the Guardia Civil and was the commander in charge of the Spanish Police operation against the 1 October referendum. As a young man, he had actively supported the failed military coup of 23 February 1981. On that day, he dressed in a blue shirt – the uniform of the fascist Falange – and volunteered at the local Guardia Civil barracks of his city of residence, Yecla.

In addition to the political control of the Constitutional Court exerted via the process of appointment of its members, the Popular Party has gone even further in damaging the arbitral role of the Court. In 2015, they used their absolute majority to revise the law regulating the Constitutional Court. This reform endowed the Constitutional Court with major executive powers, turning it, de facto, into a penal jury, the top of the judiciary system. The Court now has the power to implement its own rulings, can demand obedience and impose penalties without proper trial. No chamber of appeal exists for such decisions. To summarise, 'for the Constitutional Court to have powers to enforce its own judgments is exceptional in Europe. It is problematical in so far as it involves the Court in executive as well as judicial functions, and moreover, as shown here, potentially engages the Court in a legislative function.'[2] That is the trick for prosecuting the organisation of a referendum. Something illegal is not necessarily something criminal. As a matter of fact, organising a referendum on independence is not a crime under Spanish penal law, because it was explicitly removed from the criminal code in 2005. However, the whole criminal case against the referendum leaders has been constructed from the allegation of disobedience to the Constitutional Court – an allegation for which there is no court to appeal to. In their aim to stop the Catalan referendum, the Spanish authorities have shredded whatever was left of the arbitral role of the Constitutional Court. Without a neutral referee, Spanish institutions can no longer mediate the Catalan crisis.

It is worth pointing out that this unfortunate state of affairs in the division of powers goes essentially unchallenged by the fourth estate. In fact, there is little pluralism in the oligopoly structure of Spanish media, especially television. The communication business exhibits a notable continuity with respect to the journalistic power structures of the dictatorship. Dominant media outlets strive to uniformly transmit Spanish nationalist and authoritarian views, and are not shy in expressing explicit xenophobic anti-Catalan hostility. Critical voices are silenced, even in so called respectable newspapers, as was the case of distinguished journalist John Carlin and others who were alleged to have been fired from *El Pais* for expressing critical views on the

Catalan crisis. In a country with poor democratic culture and very low reading rates, the impact on public opinion is overwhelming.

Conclusion

We have identified four main culprits for the present political deadlock between Catalonia and Spain. First, the authoritarian context that shaped the drafting of the constitution in 1978 where Catalonia's national status was not explicitly acknowledged. Second, a system of territorial representation biased to the national majority combined with institutional arrangements where the Catalan minority has no protection from the Spanish majority. Third, the severe malfunctions in the judiciary, where Spanish political parties actively interfere, generally undermining, overriding or abolishing checks and balances, especially in high courts and in cases that relate to the Basque Country or Catalonia. Fourth, the political manipulations of the Constitutional Court, and its unusual executive powers, that have rendered this court incapable of acting as a neutral referee. Over time, the compound effect of those four factors has imposed the current dominant interpretation of the constitution that very explicitly refuses to acknowledge Catalonia's national status.

How can a national minority change its political status if the majority is intent on not allowing the minority to change it? If no central institutions of the state remain neutral to offer political guarantees, 'democracy' allows the state to nullify the rights of the national minority. But this is only sustainable through repression of dissidence and ignorance of the democratic rights of a minority.

The crux of the present political conflict is the inability of the dominant bloc of Spanish nationalism – political parties, police forces, media outlets and judicial authorities – to exercise self-restraint in order to guarantee respect for Catalans' civil rights and self-government. This failure is at the same time the main cause of the crisis and the strongest democratic argument for Catalan independence.

Bibliographical note:

Bibliographical sources in English are scarce. Bambery, C and Kerevan, G, *Catalonia Reborn: How Catalonia Took On the Corrupt Spanish State and the Legacy of Franco, Edinburgh, 2018,* includes a good overview of the Spanish transition to democracy. Guillen Lopez, E, 'Judicial Review in Spain: The Constitutional Court', in 41, Loy. L.A. L Rev 529, 2008 describes the role of the Constitutional Court. Costa, J. P., F. Tulkens, W. Kalek and J. Simor (2017) 'Catalonian Human Rights Review: Judicial Controls in the Context of the 1 October Referendum', is a legal opinion written by four leading human rights lawyers reviewing institutional malfunction and human rights violations prior to October 2017.

In Spanish, Casals, X.*La Transición española. El voto ignorado de las armas.* Barcelona, 2016, and Muniesa i Brito, B., *Dictadura y transición*, Barcelona, 2005 are thorough historical reviews of the transition to democracy, and Baby, S, *El mito de la transición pacífica. Violencia política en España (1975–1982)*, Madrid, 2018, (translated from the original French) is an extensive study of violence during the transition. Bosch, J. and Ignacio Ecolar, J, *El secuestro de la Justicia*, Barcelona, 2017, discuss political interference in the Spanish justice system.

Chapter 2

The historical background

Medieval origins and early modern identity

The historical record of Catalonia goes back to the end of the 9th century, as the heirs of Charlemagne softened their control on their territories south of Pyrénées. Initially, there was a movement toward the aggregation of counties that was led by the Count of Barcelona. The House of Barcelona, after the marriage in 1137 of Count Ramon Berenguer IV with Petronilla, the female heir of the Aragonese monarchy, became the royal family of the Aragon Crown until 1410. This realm was a confederation composed by four different countries each with their own constitutions – Aragon, Catalonia, Mallorca and Valencia. By 1410, because of lack of heirs, a new royal house was elected – Antequera, a Trastamara branch. The famous king of this dynasty was Ferdinand II, who married his cousin Isabella of Castile in 1469 and brought about the eventual unification of Castilian and Aragonese monarchies. They became known as The Catholic Monarchs. Their heritage was a common crown, but their kingdoms remained completely independent. The Habsburg monarchs of the 17th and 18th centuries were kings of Castile and of Aragon separately, and they had to swear to Catalan constitutions as well as all the constitutions of the other Aragonese kingdoms. The Cortes of Catalonia were one of the earliest European cases of a representative parliament, with precedents in previous forms of political representation. The permanent office in charge of collecting taxes and managing expenses between meetings was the Generalitat – a name for the Catalan Government that is still in use.

The golden years of the Catalan-Aragonese Crown were from the 13th to the 15th centuries, when it built and commanded a large Mediterranean empire featuring Sardinia, Sicily and Naples. During the 15th century, Catalonia suffered a series of civil wars. It came out of them politically and economically weakened, but the feudal class system had been undermined, allowing for a freer peasant society to develop. After the European centre of gravity switched from the Mediterranean to the Atlantic in the 16th century, Catalonia lost economic momentum, but was still an attractive destination for many thousands of French who settled in the sparsely populated Catalan countryside.

Catalans were self-governed for more than seven centuries. They had a distinct language that was used for all purposes – including high culture, trade, politics and public administration. But the crown union with Castile was a serious threat for all of the Aragonese territories, as Castile possessed a much larger population and a more dynamic economy from the 15th and 16th centuries as it benefited from its territorial expansion and the arrival of large quantities of gold and silver from its American colonies.

From 1640 Secession to Catalan defeat in 1714
The year 1640 marks a major divide in Catalan history and the first explosion of the kind of conflicts with Castile that have plagued Catalonia for centuries. What happened was common to many European territories that suffered under the pressure of increased taxation from their absolute monarchs to fund the conflicts of the Thirty Years War. This triggered revolutions, revolts and independence

movements in countries like England, Portugal, Naples, Andalusia, Aragon and a few years later, the Fronde, not to mention the Dutch War of Independence that also peaked around 1640.

The Count-Duke of Olivares, the de facto prime minister of King Philip IV of Castile, Aragon and many more territories, decided that the high financial needs of the Crown, that was fighting many battles all over Europe, meant that it needed more material support from the non-Castilian kingdoms. Castile had seen its representative institutions defeated by Charles I as an outcome of the 'comuneros' revolt in 1520 to 1521. Therefore, it did not pose any resistance to the King's request for more taxes. But the other kingdoms, and notably all the Aragonese territories, had strong representative institutions. The tension, growing since Philip IV became king in 1621, exploded in June 1640 in what is known as the 'Reapers' War'. A quick series of events, later also known as 'the revolt of the Catalans', brought Catalonia first to a declaration of independence in 1641, and later to seek the protection of the French crown against the Castilian king. For 12 years, Catalonia was a divided country, mostly under French rule. In 1659, 11 years after the Westphalia Treaty ended the Thirty Years War across most of Europe, Philip IV and Louis XIII of France agreed the Pyrénées Treaty which saw the Franco-Spanish frontier redrawn, and the Catalan speaking Roussillon territories on the northern side of the Pyrénées become French.

The high tension experienced between Catalonia and her King did not change the constitutional relationship between them. Catalonia remained a separate kingdom, and the new king, Charles II, crowned in 1665, pledged an oath to the Catalan constitutions. During his reign, Catalonia still suffered invasions from France. Nevertheless, the Catalan economy enjoyed economic growth based on increased trading relations with north-western Europe, mostly through spirit exports in exchange for manufactured goods. When Charles II died without a fully recognised heir, all four kingdoms of the Crown of Aragon – Aragon, Catalonia, Mallorca and Valencia – defended the claim of Archduke Charles of Habsburg in his bid for the succession to the Castilian and Aragonese Crowns, against the Bourbon Philip V, grandchild of Louis XIV of France.

The conflict became European, even global, as most of Europe was opposed to the idea of the same dynasty reigning in both France and in Castile and Aragon. Although facing defeat around much of the world, the Bourbon troops managed to triumph over their enemies in Spain. The Bourbons arrived at the Utrecht Peace Treaty in 1713 and – by accepting their losses in Europe and America – retained full control of what was becoming known as Spain, with the exceptions of Menorca and Gibraltar. Indeed, the anti-Bourbon alliance lost interest in defending the Archduke Charles as a potential King of Castile and Aragon when he became Emperor of the Holy Roman Empire. Catalonia, alongside Mallorca, were the losers in this global negotiation. They resisted for one more year in Catalonia and two more in Mallorca, but were defeated and their constitutions and institutions wiped out. For both, just as for

Aragon and Valencia in 1706 and 1707 respectively, this was their end as independent kingdoms.

Disempowered Catalonia: 1714–1808

Following the war, some 6,000 Catalans had to go into exile, mostly to Vienna. The new Spanish regime, now truly Spanish as the Aragon Crown territories were unified under Castilian administrative absolutist standards, imposed a new legal and political framework in Catalonia through the 'Nova Planta decrees' of 1716. Catalonia lost any political power. It was ruled by a Castilian administration and justice, under what was a permanent emergency regime. Catalan was forbidden as an official language. A fiscal reform was imposed that introduced direct taxation, traditionally considered to be a humiliation tactic.

For the following half century, Catalans, under Bourbon administration, were reduced to Spanish vassals under King Philip V. They had to instead turn their energies towards earning their living. These hard-working times allowed Catalans to build upon on their pre-1700 focusses on production, growing vineyards and spirit distilleries, and trade, particularly with northwestern Europe.

Things changed under Charles III, who ruled between 1759 and 1788. He was the former king of Naples, where he promoted some enlightened reforms. In 1765, he signed a, perhaps misleadingly worded, 'free trade decree' that opened direct trade between nine peninsular ports and America, replacing the previous monopoly system that had restricted trade with America to Seville and later Cádiz. The success of the measure led to a second decree in 1778 that increased the number of Spanish and American ports that could enjoy direct trade. For Catalonia, this meant the opening of Barcelona, and later Tortosa, to this new commercial system. It was very profitable, both for private interests and for the Crown treasury. The situation did not last for long, but nevertheless, Catalans grasped their opportunity. It allowed for a new era of prosperity for Catalan businesses in sectors ranging from agriculture to manufacturing and trade. The country had no political representation, but at least it enjoyed nice profits and growing wealth.

From the outbreak of the French Revolution, Spain, and particularly Catalonia as a frontier region, had to suffer a number of wars with revolutionary France. When the conflict became less revolutionary and more geopolitical, Spain had to accept a partnership with France to defend each other against British attacks. Spanish and French maritime power was crushed at the Battle of Trafalgar in 1805, and Spanish capacity to control its American Empire disappeared. The highly profitable direct trade with America collapsed too.

Catalonia was under Napoleon's rule for six years, from 1808 to 1814. It is worth mentioning than during the last two years of that period, between 1812 and 1814, Catalonia was annexed directly into the French Empire as four 'départements'. The annexation was a consequence of Catalonia's status as a critical frontier region that France had disputed with Spain for centuries and its status as an advanced manufacturing area, but also because of French understanding that they could take advantage of the long running conflict between Catalonia and Spain. Napoleon announced that the Catalan language would become co-official with French as a way to attract Catalans to his side. The two years of full integration into the French Empire had little lasting influence on Catalonia's future, but they caused alarm for Spanish rulers that Catalonia could potentially switch to the French side in the future, as it had previously after the Catalan revolt of 1640 or during various French invasions in late 17th century, or even that it could aim at independence.

Catalonia in liberal Spain: Spanish dream

Catalans had no representative mechanisms within the Bourbon monarchy. Paradoxically, the French invasion triggered one. The popular reaction against the French military, and the absence of any royal power in Spain, allowed for the emergence of a new resistance movement and the Cortes of Cádiz (the main Spanish trade port with America, which was under British navy protection during the Napoleonic wars), the first national assembly that aimed at full representation of all Spanish citizens from both the Old World and the New. In this body, Catalans could participate on the same footing as the rest of Spain. The collapse of the absolutist monarchy was the chance for Catalans to retake control of their future. They attended the Cádiz Cortes with enthusiasm and plenty of expectations. They were ready to contribute to the building of the Spanish nation or, as an alternative choice, to request the recognition of their former constitutions and institutions. The war, popular resistance to Napoleon and the democratic egalitarianism embodied in the new Spanish constitutional project – a copy of 1791 French revolutionary constitution – encouraged Catalans to decide to fully support the new nation that was developing. Even if the Cádiz Constitution was only in effect between 1812 and

1814, 1820 and 1823 and 1836 and 1837, following a series of absolutists counter-reactions, its principles offered the prospect of an equal Spanishness for all.

Indeed, even during the worst reactionary moments that followed the end of the Napoleonic era, Catalans felt they now had a national project worth their loyalty. The Catalan elites began to abandon the public use of Catalan language, even though the Catalan accent with which they spoke Castilian was seen as ridiculous in Madrid. The collapse of the Empire forced Spaniards to build a unified economy and to rely on each other. The switch from Empire to Nation was not simple at all, leading to impoverishment for all, especially for those that had previously benefited the most from the Empire. It meant a closing of access to the Spanish economy that allowed Catalan producers to gain full control of domestic markets for their manufactured goods, in exchange for a range of non-Catalan agrarian products. This marked the building of a national market. In this new economy, Catalans crafted a leading role for themselves.

It is important to remember that liberal Spanishness was not embraced by all Catalans. The Carlist movement, which saw traditionalist alternate claimants to the Spanish throne attempt to seize control of the country in a series of revolts between 1833 and 1876, was deeply rooted in Catalonia. However, they drew support less as a result of the reactionary character of Carlism, and more because they fully recognised Catalonia's historic constitutions and institutions.

An industrial revolution and a bombed city
The Catalan economy experienced an industrial revolution during the 1800s. This had deep roots in the country's early

industrialisation during the last third of the 18th century. Catalonia's 18th century industrialisation, close in many respects to Britain's experience in the same period, albeit on a smaller scale, developed in an imperial context. Even if the country mostly catered to markets within the Iberian Peninsula, a good fraction of its trade was with Spanish America. By the second third of the 19th century, American markets, with the exceptions of Cuba and Puerto Rico which remained under colonial rule, had vanished. Yet, Catalan cotton textile manufacturing tradition was so well developed by this point that it took off as soon as Spain's internal market began to grow again, with Catalan manufacturers benefitting from protectionist measures that shielded them from French and British competition. Catalans became richer as a result of their industrial advance. As the economy became more productive, they invested heavily in capital goods, first machinery and buildings and later transport infrastructure and equipment. The new Catalan industrial society became increasingly different to that of Spanish agrarian regions, and even to important Spanish cities like Madrid, Seville and Cádiz.

Because of this contrasting social structure, with Catalonia possessing a much larger urban working class in Barcelona and a number of other industrial towns, Catalan politics developed differently to those of Spain. It was more radical, democratic and pro-federalist. Electoral results contrasted starkly with the rest of Spain. With such different economic and social structures, the Catalan capital Barcelona had a different political pulse than Spain. During most of the 19th century, Barcelona was under emergency military rule. It was even bombed by the military on a number of occasions. Indeed, one well-known Spanish military chief and political leader, Espartero, authored a famous sentence: 'Barcelona has to be bombed at least once every 50 years to be kept under control'. This saying has been remembered time and again in Spanish politics, even up to the present day. Yet, the more Barcelona was bombed, the stronger its feeling of difference grew.

Catalan dynamism seemed unstoppable. Her reputation allowed political ambitions to shake traditional Spain and to attempt to change it for good. This was the destiny of Joan Prim, a Catalan general who had been one of the two military leaders of the September 1868 revolution which overthrew the monarchy of Queen Isabella II. Prim was prime minister and the person in charge of looking for a new king for Spain. After much discussion, the Italian prince Amadeo from the House of Savoy was selected. Unfortunately, Prim was assassinated in 1870, just before Amadeo's arrival in Spain. No other Catalan has since reached the pre-eminent position Prim achieved in the Spanish government.

When King Amadeo abdicated three years later, the First Spanish Republic was instituted in 1873. The Republic lasted for less than one year, but Catalans featured prominently, providing two of the four Presidents of this short lived regime. The Republic was the triumph of the periphery over the centre of Spain. It did not last, but lived long in the memory as a menace to its opponents and a hope for its supporters. The economic, social and political contrast between Catalonia and the rest of Spain put a clear brake on the Spanish dream.

Catalan Renaixença

The Renaixença ('renaissance') started in 1833 with Aribau's famous poem, in Catalan, 'Oda a la patria'. It followed a long period of decline (the 'decadència') when the Catalan language was being reduced to domestic use and Castilian had become the public language for both high and low culture. The Renaixença expanded and diffused in the 1840s and 1850s, peaking in 1859 when the annual Catalan poetry competition 'Jocs Florals' began. In the 1860s, Catalan became widely used and popular for communication and entertainment purposes, from newspapers to theatre, novels and songs, both in comic and serious settings. During the last decades of the century, the Renaixença movement developed an array of Catalan symbols: national hymn, national flag, national dance, national holiday, and so on. The Catalan-based institutions created in the 20th century would officially adopt all of these symbols. Together, they provided a well-defined sense of national identity.

Of course, all of this was happening alongside the diffusion of romanticism and nationalism, national pride and national revolutions all over Europe. These had started around 1830, peaked in 1848 and kept going until completion of German and Italian unifications around 1870.

Renaixença's social success was broad and deep, developing in parallel with the growing dissatisfaction with the course of public affairs in Spain. Industrial Catalonia found it hard to fit into Spanish politics. Catalonia was in an exceptional position in Spain, with even the Basque country not developing an industrial economy until later. The country's specialised economy contrasted with the rest of

Spain, which was oriented towards agriculture and mining. The United Kingdom's industrialisation shocked societies across both Europe and the world. It produced two different reactions: adaptation or competition. Those who decided to adapt supported their export sectors to take full advantage of Britain's openness to trade. Those who sought to compete, focussed on their industrial sectors. Castile, and Spain at large, went for the former approach, while Catalonia and the Basque Country went for the latter. Most Catalans were protectionist, most Spaniards free-traders. Catalans had an industrial bourgeoisie, Spaniards had landed elites. Most Catalans were industrial workers, most Spaniards, peasants. Most Catalans were republicans and federalists, while most Spaniards were more monarchists and unitarians. All of this became evident during the few years of universal male suffrage between 1869 and 1873. Generally speaking, the aims and ideals of Catalans were in opposition to those of Spaniards.

The rise of Catalanism and the collapse of the Spanish dream

In the intense turmoil of the revolutionary years, with a Cuban War between 1868 and 1878, a Carlist War from 1872 to 1876 and a decentralist 'cantonalist' insurrection in 1873, the son of Isabella II, Alphonse XII, had returned from exile to be crown King of Spain in 1874. He was supported by the two dynastic parties, conservatives and liberals, who alternated in government for almost half a century through fraudulent elections.

Carlists and republicans of all kinds remained on the periphery of the new regime, but in Catalonia these groups found a number of opportunities to rally in defence of Catalan rights against Spanish government centralisation, which had become more intense following the failure of Spain's first Republican experience. The politically involved generation of the 1880s, under Valentí Almirall's leadership, framed a new political paradigm. What is now known as the Catalanist movement started in the mid-1880s as a delayed consequence of Catalonia's failure to take a leading role in Spanish politics and as a reaction against the Spanish central government's policies. It was a time when expectations of further transformation and change of Spain were disappointed, and the Spanish national project started to collapse. The project of a unified civil code triggered widespread protests in defence of Catalan civil law, which had been a survivor of the 'Nova Planta' decree. The dispute around commercial policy – protectionism versus free trade – was peaking, with Catalans very much in favour of protection while Madrid and Valencia favoured free trade. In Catalonia, it meant the surge of a sense of collective identity. By 1885, a 'grievances memorandum', asking for political and cultural autonomy, was presented to the King. A first draft of a Catalan Constitution within Spain was discussed and approved by Catalanist forces in 1892. It was very much inspired by the traditional medieval and early modern Catalan constitutions.

On the other side, male universal suffrage opened political competition beyond the frontiers of the two dynastic parties, the conservatives and liberals. Republicans, Carlists, federalists, as well as disenchanted conservatives and liberals, entered strongly in local councils, Barcelona being the most important. And the foundation of Lliga Regionalista to foster Catalanist success in municipal and provincial elections started modern political Catalanism around the turn of the century.

The 1898 loss of Cuba, Puerto Rico and Philippines to the United States had a big impact in metropolitan Spain. In the Age of Empire, Spain had lost almost all of its own overseas possessions. Catalan interests were heavily involved in the Empire. The loss of Cuba was perceived as a major blow in particular. The criticism against the Spanish ruling classes was widespread all over Spain, triggering a 'regenerationist' movement. In Catalonia, it manifested itself as a widespread protest against the tax increases approved by the central government in 1899. Catalans felt aggravated, as they contributed significantly to public finances and perceived that they received nothing in exchange. The protest even led to a boycott of the Treasury, which saw many people imprisoned. Lliga Regionalista and its leader, Enric Prat de la Riba – who was imprisoned himself during these protests – started their successful political careers at this point.

A first success of Catalanism: the 'Mancomunitat'

Lliga Regionalista representatives were quite successful in their attempt to gain election to town councils. They gained ever greater success when they built a large coalition against the dynastic conservatives and liberals that included carlists and republicans. Their major breakthrough came when a united electoral list, 'Solidaritat Catalana', ran in the Spanish Congress elections of 1907. Non-dynastic Catalan parties had previously been very divided. However, they reached an agreement as a protest against a new law passed by the central government that put Catalan newspapers under military jurisdiction. The mass protests resulted in the central government imposing martial law in Barcelona. The Solidaritat Catalana list, made possible as a joint protest against these incidents, was a huge success. It won 41 out of the 44 parliamentary seats that were being contested. This new impetus beyond the movement led to demands for some sort of self-government for Catalonia. Despite some setbacks, notably those caused by the violent confrontations of the 'Tragic Week' of July 1909, the claim for some form of Catalan self-government was eventually accepted by the Canalejas liberal government in 1912. The 'Mancomunitat' (Commonwealth) did not promise self-government, but offered a Catalan authority based upon the merger of four existing provincial administrations in Catalonia. It was an immediate success, proudly engaging the new Catalan political class and mobilising of its professional, cultural and political energies into the new institutions. Many of them have lasted up to the present day.

The Mancomunitat, approved in 1913 and initiated in 1914, was only an administrative initiative. It was exploited to the full by Catalanists thanks to the administrative and political genius of Enric Prat de la Riba, the first leader of Lliga Regionalista and the first President of the Mancomunitat. He died in 1917 and was succeeded by the famous modernist architect Josep Puig i Cadafalch, who governed efficiently until 1923.

Further political recognition, beyond administrative coordination, was looked after by Catalan representatives at the Spanish Parliament. The complaints about the Spanish ruling parties – notably the disconnection between Catalan and Spanish interests and feelings – and international developments, including the First World War and Russian Revolution, all created an environment conducive to requests for self-government. The general atmosphere remained heated for several years. The fourteen points of President Wilson were extremely popular in Catalonia. The Versailles Treaty and the redrawing of European frontiers captured the imagination and the political dreams of Catalans. The creation of many new states was a promise of a brighter, independent future. From 1917, Catalan representatives asked forcefully for an Autonomy Statute. It became the political goal for all Catalan political forces, from right to left. It was believed that such a Statute would bring recognition of Catalonia as political entity.

But Catalan politics was unable to fully focus on the achievement of self-government. Many more things happened in the same period that made political life much more complex. Barcelona enjoyed great prosperity during the war years. It was the largest neutral city close to a major fighting power. All kinds of business deals were easy to close. But the return to normal life was difficult to swallow. Prices rose and wages stagnated. The Soviet revolution was a model that inspired many. As a result, a fierce class struggle developed. Both trade unions, especially the most extreme anarchists, on one side, and employers associations, particularly the most radical right-wingers, on the other, turned violent. The

State delegate, the Captain General, was actively involved in defending manufacturers and in prosecuting trade unionists. For a few long years the social and political environment was extremely tense. In September 1923, Catalonia's Captain General, Miguel Primo de Rivera, led a coup d'état and established a dictatorship. He took advantage of his new position to clamp down on anarchists and CNT trade unions and supporters of Catalan self-government. In 1924, he put the Mancomunitat under political control, and in 1925 dissolved it completely.

From failure to rebirth: Dictatorship, Republic and Independence Declaration

Primo de Rivera was ostensibly anti-Catalan. Besides closing the cherished Mancomunitat, he attacked the public use of the Catalan language. The Dictatorship enjoyed some years of economic success that triggered the first huge wave of migration from the poorer Spanish regions to Catalonia. But this could not last for long. Indeed, Primo de Rivera resigned in January 1930, and his replacement, General Berenguer, after some hesitation organised a slow transition to democracy.

Following a plan to move back to democratic government one step at a time, municipal elections were called for 12 April 1931. But both the monarchy and the military, and their supporting dynastic parties, were unaware of how distant the Spanish population was from them. On 12 April, the republican parties won a string of successes in the major towns. In response, King Alfonso XIII, abdicated and left for Rome.

As Catalans had the opportunity to vote, they asserted that they were Catalan, Republican and Left. In Barcelona, Francesc Macià, the leader of the ERC (Esquerra Republicana de Catalunya or Catalan Republican Left) a party that was created to compete in the municipal elections, won by a landslide and proclaimed the Catalan Republic within an Iberian Confederation. Macià, who had led a failed military invasion of Catalonia in 1926 and remained in exile in Brussels for some years, was the most prominent of all Catalan pro-independence politicians, as well as the most popular and well-loved. He was a romantic character, the opposite of Francesc Cambó, the Lliga's leader, a successful business-man who was well connected to Spain's business elite and was always ready to support the Spanish monarchy.

Spain's republican parties reacted quickly to the proclamation of a Catalan Republic. They managed to convince Macià to renounce the Catalan Republic and accept their commitment to approve a Statute of Autonomy for Catalonia. After long hesitations, a failed anti-republican coup and a lively parliamentary debate, the Catalan Statute of Autonomy was approved a year and a half later in September 1932.

After two years of a Republic governed by the centre and left republican parties, centre and right wing republican parties came to power in 1933. When in early October 1934 CEDA (a non-republican party that brought together a number of right wing regional parties), which was regarded with suspicion due to its suspected sympathies with the doctrines and political style of fascist dictators like Dollfuss, Mussolini and Hitler, entered into government, the socialists called for a general strike that was supported in massive numbers in the Asturias region. Lluís Companys, the new President of the Generalitat after Francesc Macià had died in 1933, proclaimed a Catalan State within the Federal Republic of Spain on 6 October. Both the Asturias general strike and the move towards Catalan independence were severely repressed. In the Catalan case, members of the government and over 3,000 people were imprisoned, judged and condemned to 30 years in jail.

In February 1936, a new general election brought the republicans and leftist parties of the Popular Front back to government. Their common goal was to free all political prisoners, which they achieved immediately after their victory.

Franco coup d'état and Autonomous Catalonia during the Civil War years

On 18 July 1936, General Francisco Franco led the military insurrection against the Republic. He quickly took full control of Spanish Morocco, the Canary and the Balearic Islands, alongside Old Castile, Navarre and Seville. But the rebellion failed in most of Spain's big cities. As a result, the coup quickly developed into a Civil War. As Franco had better organisation, a clear purpose and active international supporters in the form of the German and Italian governments and some large British and American companies, he managed to turn the war in his favour.

The rebels mobilised those that felt menaced by the republican agrarian reform, by secular religious reforms, by the approval of autonomy statutes for Catalonia, the Basque

Country and Galicia, and by the ever more influential trade unions. In Catalonia, the new republican regime, the Generalitat government, promoted action on four fronts: agrarian reform, political self-government including protection of the Catalan language, education and culture, a secular approach to religious affairs, and protection of trade union rights. Catalonia's autonomous governments during these years were led by ERC, who enjoyed large parliamentary majorities in every election between 1931 and 1936.

On 18 July Barcelona and Catalonia remained loyal to the Republic. Anarchists and CNT members secured firearms from military barracks, defeated those that wanted to follow Franco's call and tried to assure the survival of the Republic. Although the Catalan government remained mostly in hands of the ERC, CNT members joined it alongside members of the socialist UGT trade union and the PSUC, which had been formed by a merger between Catalonia's socialists and communists. Until May 1937, the Catalan government was de facto independent from the rest of Spain – an experience that left bitter feelings in Madrid and mixed ones in Barcelona. After May, when communists managed to exclude Trotskyists and anarchists from power, the government became closely aligned with Spain's national republican government. Nevertheless, Barcelona was occupied by the Francoists on 26 January 1939 and the war was finally ended on 1 April, with complete victory for Franco. The republican dream of resisting until the outbreak of a new world war had not been achieved.

The Civil War of 1936 to 1939 was devastating, especially for those who had been defeated. Catalonia lost in a number of key ways. The leftist parties and trade unions were defeated and prohibited, just as in the rest of Spain. The internal conflict within the republican side was disastrous for the Catalan war effort, and for the forging of any opposition consensus after Franco's occupation. The Catalan-based parties were prohibited and ferociously repressed. This was a different experience to the rest of Spain that was only comparable to the Basque Country, but with a difference in that Catalonia had resisted Franco for far longer than the Basque Country. Catalonia's main governing party, the ERC, was badly hit. Companys, the ERC's Generalitat President, was killed by Franco in 1940 following a quick military trial. The ERC, that had managed to put together governments with republicans, anarchists, socialists and communists, represented all the evils that Franco hated the most: Catalan separatists, 'reds' and freemasons. On the right wing of Catalan society, the Lliga Catalana, formerly the Lliga Regionalista, had been the leading party. They mostly supported Franco's coup d'état, but they had reacted more slowly to support his rebellion than many others and always remained under suspicion of Catalanism in the eyes of the dictator. The true supporters of Franco were few in Catalonia, although they grew in number during the war after anarchists began to shoot priests, Catholics, businessmen, capitalists and political opponents. This shortage of domestic political support opened the way for many Franco enthusiasts to settle in Catalonia after the war.

Franco's long-lasting repression

Franco regime lasted for over 36 years, from 1939 to 1975. It completely destroyed Catalan institutions and political autonomy. For decades, it persecuted Catalan language and culture. It executed some 4,000 Catalans, had many more in jail for years and forced around 100,000 into exile, including all republican Catalan authorities. Political repression was particularly ferocious during the Second World War years, but it never stopped. The last executions of the Franco regime took place at the end of September 1975, two months before his death.

In the meantime, Catalonia was completely transformed. Initially, Franco was extremely hostile to everything Catalan. During the years in which he pursued a policy of autarchy, attempting to close off the Spanish economy from the outside world, he designed a plan to deindustrialise Catalonia and force Catalan entrepreneurs and capitalists to invest in the rest of Spain. But as the gap between stagnant and hungry Spain and the increasingly prosperous postwar Western European world reached intolerable levels, with Spain's GDP per capita relative to Western Europe dropping from 67.3 per cent of the Western European average in 1935, to 52.9 in 1950 and 50.8 in 1960, Franco eventually allowed Catalans to develop their own businesses. This started in the 1950s, and grew more widespread from around 1960. After two decades of economic crisis, destruction and depression and repression, any positive incentive could have a major impact. Indeed, for almost a quarter of a century, the Catalan economy grew rapidly, and received more than 1.5 million immigrants from poorer Spanish regions. This was equivalent to half of the Catalan population of 1940 arriving in the country. This was a major demographic change, difficult to accommodate properly due to the exceptional political circumstances of the period. Catalonia's position within Spain rose in terms of both its overall population and GDP although its average income per capita relative to the rest of Spain declined as the Basque Country and Madrid overtook – yet even so it remained well above the Spanish average.

By the end of the Franco era, Catalonia was a very industrial region with a large working class of mostly non-Catalan origin. Cities were in an awful state, due to a lack of urban planning and public services. Income inequality was high. New resistance to the Franco regime was growing among university students, illegal trade unions and the emerging middle classes. They complained of absence of all kinds of freedom and of tough political repression. The former republican and anarchist resistance, the leading social and political movements during the Second Republic, were very weak following their repression in the aftermath of the Civil War. The Franco regime lasted long enough to force a major demographic change both among the population at large and among the political and cultural elites.

A window of opportunity: Transition years

Although repression was pervasive, some coordination among political opposition forces allowed for the emergence of the 'Assemblea de Catalunya' (Catalonia's Assembly) that gathered together all those opposing Franco's regime in 1971. In the lead up to the transition to democracy, they successfully organised demonstrations under the slogan 'Freedom, Amnesty and Statute of Autonomy'.

Once Franco died on 20 November 1975, events developed quickly. King Juan Carlos I was crowned on 22 November. Although he ratified the last of Franco's prime ministers into office, he replaced him in early July 1976, naming the then unknown Adolfo Suárez in his place. Suárez initiated the transition: presenting a referendum to change Franco's constitutional laws, agreeing to the recognition of most opposition parties, including communists, but excluding independentists like the ERC, and announcing democratic elections on 15 June 1977.

The first democratic elections produced quite different results in Catalonia than in Spain, where the centre-right UCD coalition supporting Adolfo Suárez clearly led the way. In Catalonia instead, out of 47 seats, the socialist PSC got 15, the nationalists lead by Jordi Pujol got 11, UCD secured 9, the communists 8, 2 were won by a coalition of Christian Democrats and liberals, 1 to the Esquerra Catalana (a front for the ERC) and 1 to Franco's heirs in the Alianza Popular. The Catalan-based parties got a clear majority of 37 out of 47 seats, while there was also a majority for left wing parties. As a direct consequence of these results, the Spanish Prime Minister Adolfo Suárez successfully negotiated the re-establishment of Catalan self-government with the Catalan republican President in exile Josep Tarradellas. The Generalitat de Catalunya was then re-established on 29 September 1977, and Tarradellas returned to Barcelona as its President.

The major political task of the newly elected Spanish Congress was the drafting of a new Constitution, its parliamentary discussion and approval, and its endorsement by the public through a referendum held on 6 December 1978. Only some of the direct heirs of the Franco Regime, the Alianza Popular that later developed into the current Popular Party, opposed or did not approve all of these reforms. Yet they were a tiny minority, with just 16 MPs out of a total of 350. The Spanish Constitution allowed Catalonia quick access to an autonomous regional government and her consideration as a 'nationality', although not a 'nation' with full sovereign rights, but more than a 'region'. The Spanish Constitution was approved in Catalonia by 90.5 per cent on a turnout of 67.9 per cent, slightly higher than in the rest of Spain. After the approval of the Constitution, Suárez called for general elections which he duly won, coming near a majority of seats.

Catalan history seemed to have reached a safe harbour when its statute of autonomy, the Catalan self-government charter, was approved in 1979, and Jordi Pujol was elected President in March 1980.

The statute of autonomy represented the recognition of political and institutional continuity with the Republican Generalitat. On paper, it allowed for a major transfer of powers from the central government to the Catalan Generalitat. It took more than one year to prepare its draft, to have it discussed at the Spanish Congress, to have it approved in a referendum, held in Catalonia on 25 October 1979, and to have it ratified by the Spanish Congress and Senate, and finally by the King. The Catalan version was published on 31 December 1979. The statute was approved by over 88 per cent on a 60.5 per cent turnout. Political support was strong, with almost all Catalan representatives at the Spanish Congress voting in favour.

A democratic Spain, with a democratic Constitution, popularly accepted in Catalonia, and a statute of autonomy, also widely approved. What built such broad ranging consensus? A widespread willingness to turn the page on Franco's Spain. When Franco died on 20 November 1975, it was clear that he was in full command of Spain. It was also clear that Spaniards were looking for political solutions that were close to those in the rest of Western Europe – a democratic regime. Indeed, a good part of Franco's supporters were convinced that their allegiance to the dictator did not prevent them from building a more consensual political solution for Spain. The very positive expectations of becoming politically, socially, culturally and economically Europeanised, was at the heart of the process known in Spain as the 'democratic transition'. The political forces opposing Franco's regime, and those who had supported Franco but were willing to switch to a European democratic model, reached quick agreements, based on a democratic political system, but also on the acceptance of the Monarchy, a united Spain, and the complete forgiveness, or amnesty, of any previous political actions that were or could be considered illegal. This allowed for the freeing of all political prisoners, but it also was a strong insurance for Franco supporters against potential changes of mood against them. The active role played by Catalonia in opposing Franco's regime, as well as her cultural and political leadership, combined with the first electoral outcomes and President Tarradellas's ability to choose the proper moment and the proper stance to negotiate his return and the restoration of Catalan self-government, made possible the road to a new statute of autonomy.

****

In this chapter we have covered the complex historical roots of this seemingly happy conclusion. 'Seemingly', as police attacks on citizens aiming to vote in an independence referendum on 1 October 2017 and the suspension of Catalan government on 27 October followed by the imprisonment or exile of all its members has given many a sense of déja vu, of Catalan history repeating itself one more time. Catalan resistance to Spanish centralisation and uniformity have time and again triggered an aggressive backlash from the latter rather than negotiation. The recognition of national differences within Spain seems hopeless.

Bibliographical note:

There are English language books written or translated that summarise Catalan history. An enjoyable Catalan history (even if the title is misleading) up to early 20th century is Hughes, R, *Barcelona*, New York, 1992. Two standard summaries are Sobrequés, J, *History of Catalonia*, Barcelona, 2007, and Cardona, F X H, *The History of Catalonia*, Barcelona, 2007. The oldest attempt is Trueta, J, *The Spirit of Catalonia*, Oxford, 1946, although it focuses on Catalan culture and institutions during the Middle ages. Modern scholars have enormously enhanced our knowledge of these founding centuries: Sabaté, F, ed., *The Crown of Aragon: a singular Mediterranean empire*, Leiden, 2017. For the early Modern period the classical reference is Elliott, J H, *The Revolt of the Catalans: A study in the decline of Spain (1598–1640)*, Cambridge, 1963. Eliott's recent *Scots and Catalans: Union and Disunion*, New Haven and London, 2018, is an excellent comparative review, but turns surprisingly partisan in its discussion of the more recent events. Major books on the history of Catalan nationalism are Balcells, A, *Catalan nationalism: past and present*, London, 1996;

McRoberts, K, *Catalonia. Nation Building Without A State*, Oxford and New York, 2001, and Smith, A, *The Origins of Catalan Nationalism, 1770–1898*, Basingstoke, 2014. An unsympathetic view of Catalan nationalism is Tortella, G *Catalonia in Spain: history and myth*, Basingstoke, 2017. Other authors have been interested by its survival and renaissance after the Civil War: Guibernau, M, *Catalan Nationalism: Francoism, transition and democracy*, Abingdon, 2004, and Dowling, A, *Catalonia Since the Spanish Civil War: Reconstructing the Nation*, Eastbourne, 2014. The Generalitat de Catalunya has made various attempts to summarise Catalan history in English. The last and more complete is Grau, R, and Muñoz, J M, eds., *Catalonia, a European History*, Barcelona, 2006.

2

Chapter 3

The story of a constitutional disagreement

The model of territorial organisation developed in the Spanish Constitution of 1978 resulted from the uneasy and, seen from the rear mirror, unsuccessful, attempts made to accommodate very diverse political preferences both in the explicit recognition of several nations (or as the final article 2 of the constitutional text established, 'nationalities and regions') within Spain and on the way to organise the distribution of competences between the central government and the regional autonomies.

At the time when the constitution was being developed, the Spanish legislature included, broadly speaking, three positions on the territorial question. Representatives from Alianza Popular, the political party that incorporated former Francoist governing authorities and that was later refounded as the current Partido Popular, as well as some non-partisan senators appointed by the King fully opposed the political recognition of any other unit aside from Spain as a nation and defended a strongly centralised state. At the other extreme of the political spectrum, the representatives of Catalan and Basque parties demanded that the constitution acknowledged the composite multi-national nature of Spain. Still, their positions were diverse, ranging from Catalan and Basque secessionist parties that, seeing Spain as a state composed of several nations, opposed the use of the term Spanish 'nation', to Catalan and Basque nationalists that, taking a more eclectic position, rejected any language stressing any national unitary features in the constitution. Finally, a broad middle-of-the-road coalition of centre-right and socialist deputies strove to reconcile calls for recognition of the pluralism and diversity of Spain with a strong commitment to the country's unity.

Although pro-centralisation deputies and senators were at that time a small minority, constitutional negotiations were strongly influenced by both the presence of old Francoist institutions and politicians and the implicit threat of intervention by the Spanish army. To secure their acquiescence to the process of democratisation, the 1977 Law of Amnesty promoted by Suárez had granted full immunity to army and police officers for crimes committed during Franco's regime. In addition, article 8 of the new constitution entrusted the Spanish army not only with the task of defending Spain's territorial integrity, as is the case in other constitutional systems, but also with the mandate of defending the constitutional order itself, a power that comes directly from the Francoist legal order.

To reconcile the rather heterogeneous preferences represented in the Cortes and, more importantly, to minimise any sabre rattling – 'ruido de sables' – from the military, Adolfo Suárez, the President of the Spanish government, imposed a loosely written definition of the territorial structure of Spain in article 2, which read as follows: 'The Constitution is based on the indissoluble unity of the Spanish Nation, the common and indivisible homeland of all Spaniards; it recognises and guarantees the right to self-government of the nationalities and regions of which it is composed and the solidarity among them all'. In other words, the article, and hence the constitution, included a strong defence of the unity of the Spanish nation and avoided the idea of a 'nation of nations' demanded by Basques and Catalans. However, to please those who did not accept the term 'region', it included the term 'nationalities'.

Interpreted literally, article 2 put both the Spanish nation and the autonomy of nationalities and regions at the same hierarchical level. However, the very early jurisprudence of the Constitutional Court interpreted that provision as placing the principle of unity and the State above self-government and the autonomous communities. Such an interpretation was conditioned by the extreme political instability of the times, the threat of military intervention, shown in the failed coup of 1981, and the system of election of the members of the Constitutional Court that disregarded national minorities.

Tensions between autonomy and recentralisation

Title Eight of the constitution, articles 137 to article 158, established the general structure of the system of distribution of competences between the central state and the so-called 'autonomous communities' in which regions were expected to organise and govern themselves. However, the lack of clarity in that system of distribution, which mirrored the ambiguities of article 2 and which has been reinforced by its subsequent interpretation and development, has caused many political controversies, considerable legal uncertainty, and countless conflicts of competences.

The first period of the constitutional development of the system of autonomous communities, through the approval of their respective 'statutes' of autonomy, in Spain took place from 1979 to 1983. A statute of autonomy is the norm that establishes the organisational structure of the autonomous Community, determines the powers it assumes, and sets the procedures through which the activity is going to be performed. It is important to emphasize that the statute of autonomy is a sub-state constitution and that, in principle, the central state cannot affect it once it is passed, except through a constitutional amendment.

That initial 'statuent period' became a decisive stage in terms of setting the number of regions, their relationship with the central state, and the mechanisms to finance the regions. Both the Basque and the Catalan statutes were approved in 1979. The negotiation strategy to get the Catalan statute approved was an episode of compromise via ambiguity. Consequently, the legislative and regulatory boundaries between the Catalan and Central jurisdictions were notably fuzzy. Under the 1979 Statute, Catalonia could aspire to administrative decentralisation, legislative powers and spending capacity in culture, education, health and social services. But the central government kept for itself tax collection and the allocation of fiscal revenues, and the last word on all essential policy making.

The ambiguity in the constitution and the statute did leave doors open, but the Spanish side soon gave signs of wanting to close them. Although the rest of Spain's regions did not initially mobilise to achieve political autonomy, the passage of the Catalan statute prompted a broad movement to pass similar laws to emulate Catalonia's self-government. By demanding the same political status as Catalonia, the Basque Country and Galicia, they challenged the seemingly initial plan of the Spanish government to recognise some asymmetric treatment between those three regions and the rest of Spain. Moreover, national politicians feared that the generalisation of a process of decentralisation would dismantle the power of the central state.

The attempted coup of February 1981 was interpreted as the signal that the armed forces would not tolerate a special treatment for Catalans and Basques. Following the failed coup, the two main Spanish parties, the centre-right UCD and the leading socialist opposition, the PSOE, signed the so-called Autonomic Pacts, which excluded the political representatives of the Basque Country and Catalonia, to 'rationalise' the territorial organisation of Spain. From that moment onward, the agenda and electoral interests of those two nationwide parties determined the evolution of the system of autonomies.

Following those pacts, the Spanish government attempted to harmonise the territorial distribution of powers, enacting the Organic Law of Harmonisation of the Autonomic Process (hereafter LOAPA for its acronym in Spanish) in 1981 and another organic law, the Organic Law 8/1980 of 22 September of the Finances of the Autonomous Communities (hereafter LOFCA for its acronym in Spanish), and the law of inter-territorial compensation fund, setting the bases of the financial autonomy and the enforcement of the solidarity principle.

The LOAPA embodied the principle of 'café para todos' (coffee for all), an expression used by Manuel Clavero Arévalo, Spanish minister of the Regions during the transitional period, to signal the need to treat everybody equally and, in the process, water down the autonomy granted to the old historical communities. Catalonia was 'equalised' to La Rioja, Cantabria or Murcia. The notion that historical nations were to get genuine self-government was rejected.

The Basque Country and Catalonia challenged the constitutionality of the LOAPA before the Constitutional Court, and 14 of its 38 articles were declared unconstitutional. This provided some damage control; the Constitutional Court reaffirmed that the statutes of autonomy were, as part of the block of constitutionality, necessary norms, jointly with the Constitution, to determine the powers of autonomous communities. But from that point onward, and in spite of this particular ruling of the constitutional court, the non-original reading of the constitution that gives priority to unity over self-government has been used as a legal alibi to institutionalise more recentralisation, harmonisation and homogenisation.

Since 1981, central governments stopped any significant decentralisation measures, trying to reinforce central powers vis-à-vis regional governments in a systematic way. This recentralisation agenda was only counteracted when the Spanish party in government needed the support of Catalan parties to form a majority in the Spanish Congress.

The recentralisation agenda found a unique opportunity to intensify in the wake of the economic crisis that started in 2008, when Madrid took advantage of measures taken to stimulate economic activity, important in a period of crisis, and to comply with the norms imposed by the European Union to enact and enforce provisions in matters that belong to the sphere of competences of the autonomous communities. Nevertheless, not all the recentralisation measures adopted by the state from 2008 to 2010 had an economic motivation – many were founded on the political and ideological conviction that the process of decentralisation had gone too far. The measures enacted by the national government to interfere in the regional competences of the autonomous communities included targeting the latter's financial autonomy, their administrative and institutional self-organisation, and the development/design of public policies.

The process to recentralise and void powers of the autonomous communities did not stop with the end of the economic crisis. On the contrary, it was reinforced through new mechanisms and legislative techniques. The emergence of new competences at the central level that interfered with regional powers ended up strengthening the position of the central administration. A key mechanism to achieve that outcome was the manipulation the European Union requirements on spending restrictions and economic stability. For example, in the Stability Plan program, sent to the European Union, the Spanish authorities agreed to eliminate a set of regional agencies that, according to them, duplicated national institutions.

Fishing in the Spanish Coffee Pot, 1980–2004

After the first election to the re-established Catalan Parliament under the new Catalan Statute in 1980, the nationalist centre, forming a minority government under President Jordi Pujol, set out to deploy Catalan self-rule from scratch. Pujol's skill at developing political and financial capacities in an institutional scenario of blurred jurisdictional boundaries and total lack of taxation capacity was remarkable in the eyes of the Catalan voters.

After his narrow victory in 1980, Pujol went on to win 4 straight elections to the Catalan Parliament and his coalition, Convergència i Unió (CIU), held the Catalan Autonomous government until 2003.

These were decades of continuous jurisdictional conflict and bargaining over the distribution of tax revenues. CIU's negotiation strategy was to trade their MP's votes in Congress – whenever they were pivotal – in exchange for small concessions that would allow gains in self-government. This step-by-step strategy of small jurisdictional and financial gains became popularly known as 'peix al cove' (fish in the bag) politics. Negotiations were messy, lengthy and contrived. Still, results were visible: a public education system where Catalan was the language of instruction and a high quality health system with universal coverage were put in place. The Catalan public television and radio sender were launched. A Catalan police force was deployed, effectively giving police control to the Catalan Government. Over time, Madrid had 'transferred' education, culture, health, social services, traffic, police, prisons and more to Barcelona. At the same time, the political interference of the central government was continuous and much energy of the Catalan institutions was spent in messy jurisdictional conflicts. A large fraction of public expenses, and policy responsibility, had been transferred, but tax collection remained almost entirely under the control of the central tax authority. There were incremental gains in transfer revenues, but they did not keep up with the pace of increased policy responsibility. The initial status quo was very unfavourable and, in the 'Coffee for all' negotiation regime, gains from there were very difficult.

There was, therefore, a chronic financial under-provision. It was not unusual for Madrid to renege on agreed deals.

The regime of territorial (re)distribution put in place to finance the 17 Autonomous communities was dysfunctional from the beginning and did not improve. Catalonia's fraction of the transfers was not in proportion to tax contributions, not even to population. Overall the system was cumbersome, subject to manipulation, and inefficient. Although the accounting is opaque and the data not easily accessible, the evaluation of the inter-territorial fiscal balances have been found disproportionately unfavourable to Catalonia. The fraction of taxes that Catalans pay to the central government but do not return as expenses in Catalonia, the fiscal deficit, is estimated at about 8.5 per cent of its GDP per year. Nowhere in OECD countries with federal system – Australia, Germany, the US – is territorial tax re-distribution of similar proportions.

Furthermore, Madrid kept the regulatory control and investment expenditure of basic public infrastructures such as main roads, trains, ports and airports, energy and telecommunications. The promoted model is radial, with a unique centre in Madrid. Underinvestment in Catalonia has been systematic.

Last but not least, conflicts over Catalan public media and education were prevalent. Hostility towards the Catalonia's distinct personality, expressed most visibly by their language, had clearly not died away, and the Catalan cultural exception remained contested by Spanish authorities, and by the median voter who elected them.

Fish in the bag politics within the 'coffee for all' regime remained successful as long as new political capacities and resources were accruing into the jurisdiction of the Catalan government, and as long as the imbalance between expense responsibility and revenues did not become too obvious. But the structural faults in the fiscal arrangement were bound to reveal that this strategy had hit its limits. The Popular Party led the Spanish government between 1997 and 2004 under President José M Aznar. Catalan fishing had been plentiful in their first term, when CiU votes had been crucial for Aznar: the police and prisons were transferred under a very flexible interpretation of the Constitution. However, once Aznar controlled Spanish Congress with an absolute majority in the second term, fishing was over. The Spanish government agenda was openly re-centralist. The prospect of bringing Catalan self-government forward was totally exhausted by the systematic interference of Spanish government laws and regulations, and political capacity was severely limited by the financial suffocation.

The reformed Catalan Statute of Autonomy

In 2003, the PSC formed a left coalition government in Catalonia along with the ERC and ICV, and left CiU as the opposition for the first time in 23 years. A main point of their joint government programme was the reform the statute of autonomy. The PSOE won the Spanish elections soon after. In the heat of the electoral campaign, socialist leader Zapatero had promised his support to whatever statute reform the Catalan Parliament approved. The Catalan tripartite coalition saw an opportunity to attempt to put self-government back on track.

The new statute, which received the support of almost 90 per cent of all the members of the Catalan Parliament, proclaimed, in its preamble, that 'Catalonia´s self-government is founded on the Constitution' but 'also on the historical rights of the Catalan people, which, in the frame-work of the Constitution, give rise to recognition in this Statute of the unique position of the Catalan Government'. Article 1 of the Statute stated that 'Catalonia, as a nation, exercises its self-government by constituting itself as an Autonomous Community'. Article 3 declared that 'the rela-tions between the Catalan government (Generalitat) and the State are founded on the principle of mutual institu-tional loyalty and are governed by the principle of auton-omy, that of bilateralism and also that of multilateralism'. Article 5 asserted that Catalan self-government was also founded on the historic rights of the Catalan people. In short, the new statute redefined the relationship between Catalonia and Spain as one inspired by the principles of national pluralism and territorial asymmetry that had inspired the constitution originally.

In general terms, the statute of autonomy pursued the following goals: i) the integrity of the competences of the Catalan Government and the autonomy of its exercise, ii) a new relationship with the State based on a reinforced bilateral relation, iii) a fair and better financial system for Catalonia, and iv) the national recognition of Catalonia and the guarantee of its essential identity elements (language, linguistic rights, own law)'.

Following constitutional procedure, which required the approval of the statute by both the Catalan and the

Spanish legislatures and by Catalan voters in a referendum, the statute was submitted to the Spanish Congress in November 2005. On 30 March 2006, after substantially amending the original law passed by the Catalan Parliament, the Spanish Congress approved the statute of autonomy of Catalonia with 189 votes in favour, 154 votes against and 2 abstentions. After the Senate passed it too, the draft was brought back to Catalonia to be ratified in a referendum on 18 June 2006. It was approved by a 73.2 per cent of the electors. But the turnout was a low 48.9 per cent, already a sign of disappointment with the whole process.

The statute reform had been received with much hostility all over Spain, right from the start. There were calls to boycott Catalan products and the PP – with Mariano Rajoy now installed as its leader – launched a nationwide campaign that collected 4 million signatures against the reform. Following its approval, the Partido Popular, the Spanish ombudsman, as well as some autonomous communities challenged the new statute before the Constitutional Court. The Constitutional Court took four years to decide on the lawsuit. The decision, which took place in the midst of an extremely antagonistic campaign from the Spanish media and the Spanish right, was split six to four and included very extensive dissenting votes that disagreed radically with the position of the majority. In addition, the legitimacy of the Court suffered from the fact that the mandates of several of its magistrates had expired and that their successors had not been chosen after the Popular Party systematically vetoed any candidate.

In an extensive ruling that stretched over 137 paragraphs, and using a strong apodictic tone and a pre-emptive strategy, the Court rejected the most significant provisions of the statute. Provisions similar to those invalidated in the Catalan Statute of Autonomy were not considered unconstitutional when included in other autonomy laws. More importantly, the constitutional court overreached by imposing its solution over the joint decision of the Catalan Parliament and the Spanish Congress (both of them the 'loci', as it were, of the Spanish and Catalan sovereigns) even though there had not been any breach in the approval procedure established by the constitution to approve the statute. The Court decision broke the constitutional pact that considered the statutes of autonomy as provisions within the block of constitutionality and ratified the process of homogenisation, centralisation and symmetry conducted through individual norms.

The decision of the constitutional court on the statute of autonomy of 2006 is arguably the most important decision issued on the territorial organisation of Spain. Forty years after the approval of the last Spanish Constitution, the 'territorial question' remains more open than ever. The 'Autonomic State' has collapsed, dragging down with it the prestige of the Constitutional Court, an institution that has been politically manipulated, undermining its role as independent and fair referee, and jeopardising the democratic principles and fundamental values enshrined by the constitution.

Bibliographical note:

On Spanish modern constitutionalism and territorial organisation, (*in Spanish*) Entrena Cuesta, R. in Garrido Falla et al, *Comentarios a la Constitución*, Madrid, 2001, and Capella, J.R *Las sombras del sistema constitucional español*, Madrid 2003. In relation to the tensions between autonomy and recentralisation in the Spanish constitutional system, see (*in Spanish*), Rubio Caballero, J.A. 'Los Nacionalistas Vascos y Catalanes ante la LOAPA: Ajustes y Desajustes en los inicios del Estado de las autonomías', *Historia Actual Online*, 2004, and Pérez Royo, J. 'Reflexiones sobre la Contribución de la Jurisprudencia Constitucional a la Construcción del Estado Autonómico', *Revista de Estudios Políticos*, 1986. On the same topic, (*in Catalan*) see Viver Pi-Sunyer, C. and Martín, G. *El procés de recentralització de l'Estat de les autonomies* Barcelona 2012 and of the same authors, *Tres informes de l'Institut d'estudis Autonòmics, el Pacte Fiscal, les Duplicitats i les Consultes Populars, Barcelona*, 2013.

On territorial fiscal flows, Bosch, N., Espasa, M. i Solé-Ollé, A. (eds.), *The political economy of inter-regional fiscal flows: measurement, determinants, and effects on country stability*, London, 2010; Paluzie, E. 'Fiscal issues of Catalan independence' in Nagel, K-J. i Rixen, S. *Catalonia in Spain and Europe. Is There a Way to Independence*, Baden-Baden, 2015, and Bel, G, *Infrastructure and the Political Economy of Nation Building in Spain, 1720–2010*. Eastbourne, 2012.

On the process of amendment of the Catalan statute of Autonomy and the effects on Spanish constitutionalism, see: Gardner, J A, and Ninet, A A, 'Sustainable Decentralisation: Power, Extraconstitutional Influence, and Subnational Symmetry in the United States and Spain', *American Journal of Comparative Law*, 2011 and of the same authors, 'Distinctive Identity Claims in Federal Systems: Judicial policing of Subnational Variance', *International Journal of Constitutional Law*, 2016. See also (*in Catalan*) Albertí Rovira, E. et al. 'La Sentència 31/2010: Valoració General del seu impacte sobre l'estatut i l'Estat de les Autonomies', in *Revista Catalana de Dret Públic*, 2010.

Chapter 4

Voters and parties march towards independence

At the turn of the century, Catalonia was regarded overall as a very stable region, with moderate politics and a generally peaceful accommodation as part of Spain. The autonomy granted by the 1978 Constitution allowed the dominant, moderate Catalan nationalists to develop self-governing institutions within Spain. Despite occasional institutional tensions that tend to occur in almost any multi-level political system, the system was generally unchallenged. Often, the Catalan case was put in contrast with the Basque Country, a much more unstable and polarised political system, in which the pervasiveness of political violence and radical pro-independence parties conditioned the development of autonomy.

But today, the population of Catalonia is polarised with about half of the electorate supporting independence while the other half is against it. Political polarisation is aggravated by repression. During the December 2017 Catalan election, and the April 2019 Spanish election, several leaders campaigned from either jail or exile. With the leaders of the 1 October referendum in prison or exile, and many other criminal cases open, supporters of independence have their civil rights threatened.

How did things get there? How and why has independence become the central issue of contention in Catalan politics? Despite the fact that a majority of Catalans traditionally favoured further autonomy, support for full independence had been rather limited until 2010. However, between 2010 and 2013, voters experienced a rapid and intense realignment of preferences, leading to about half of the electorate moving towards explicit support for independence.

Since 2013, positions have crystallised and both the pro- and anti-independence camps have become increasingly entrenched and intensely mobilised.

We argue that this has been a bottom up movement, where the civil society and grassroots organisations of the pro-independence movement have played a leading role, pushing Catalan political parties to adjust their agendas. This has caused a major disruption in the electoral landscape and the political party system of Catalonia, and has brought about a major conflict with Spanish institutions that may lead to Catalonia separating from the Kingdom of Spain.

The reasons behind the surge in support for independence

While for many in the international arena the Catalan pro-independence demands are new, secessionist groups have existed in Catalonia for at least the last 100 years. However, for the larger part of that period, explicitly pro-independence positions were never dominant within Catalan nationalism.

This is especially true for the post-Francoist period. Ever since the restoration of democracy in 1978, mainstream Catalan nationalism has sought compromise with Spain in order to achieve a gradual increase in devolved powers, rather than full separation. Even the parties that had self-determination and independence in their manifestos took part in the compromise strategy, and sought negotiations for increased autonomy.

This was congruent with the preferences of the population. When asked by the CEO, the Catalan Centre for Opinions, about their preferred constitutional arrangement in 2006, only 14 per cent of respondents chose secession as their first preference among four options – centralisation, status quo, federalism or secession. However, when the same poll repeated the question in 2013, the number had skyrocketed to 48.5 per cent, stabilising later on around 40 per cent. When asked directly about their vote in a potential referendum, around 50 per cent declared that they would favour independence.

However, this abrupt change obscures a more stable feature of Catalan public opinion: even if often falling short of demanding full independence, a majority of Catalan citizens have favoured full decentralisation ever since autonomous institutions were restored. This widespread demand for more autonomy was already over 60 per cent in 2002, according to a survey fielded by the Spanish governments' Sociological Research Institute (CIS). Since then, those that believe that Catalonia has an insufficient level of autonomy have stood at around around 65 per cent of the population, according to the CEO surveys.

This is crucial, because it sets the preconditions for the shift towards secessionism. In 2005, the Catalan Parliament had passed the proposed reform of the Statute of Autonomy, and as we have discussed in Chapter 3 the response of both the PSOE and PP to this caused great frustration for Catalan voters. President José Luís Rodríguez Zapatero reneged on his promise to support it, imposing major amendments for its approval in the

Spanish Congress. Rajoy, then leading the PP, challenged the Statute before the Spanish Constitutional Court, which four years later ruled against key parts of the text, thus further limiting autonomy.

That ruling of the Constitutional Court is often regarded as a key tipping point for the evolution of demands for independence in Catalonia. Moreover, it was further aggravated by the recentralisation strategy that the Popular Party implemented after it formed a government in 2011. Taking advantage of the Great Recession, the Rajoy government imposed a tight financial control on the autonomous communities that, in practice, suppressed any remaining financial autonomy.

These episodes – from the amendments and later ruling against the Statute of Autonomy passed by the Catalan Parliament, to the recentralisation policies set up by the PP government between 2011 and 2018 – illustrate a core concern for those that support Catalan self-government: the lack of guarantees in the Spanish constitutional framework. The state institutions, from the executive to the legislature and the judiciary, have ample margin to limit and water down the powers of the Catalan government and parliament. One of the goals of the 2005 statute passed by the Catalan Parliament was to set a system of guarantees to protect their autonomy from central interference, but that was rejected by the central power.

In the wake of the Constitutional Court decision and the Popular Party policies, the segment of the population that wanted further decentralisation faced a stark dilemma: either accept the status quo of limited, decreasing and insecure autonomy, or shift to a more radical demand for self-determination and full independence from Spain. This explains why a growing number of federalists started to support the idea of separation.

If we order the constitutional preferences in a continuum between full centralisation and full independence, the bulk of the electorate has for a long time been located somewhere in between the status quo and full independence. However, as the status quo moved backwards, towards recentralisation, these voters found themselves gradually moving closer to independence than to the status quo. Therefore, it is hardly surprising that a substantial proportion shifted towards independence, as illustrated by Figure 1.

How can we explain this realignment in such a short period of time? Alternative explanations have been put forward.

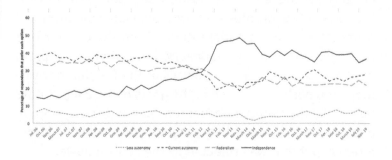

Fig. 1

Constitutional preferences in Catalonia, 2006–18
(Source: CEO)

The first one links the pro-independence movement to the general reaction to the financial crisis that was especially acute in Southern Europe. During the period of 2008 to 2014, the rate of unemployment in Catalonia and support for independence were strikingly parallel.

In a general sense, one could argue that the crisis did indeed play a role. First, it provided the Spanish government with the opportunity to pursue a recentralisation of financial powers. Second, we have some evidence that some of the new supporters of independence were motivated by instrumental concerns related to the negative net fiscal flows between Catalonia and Spain, and infrastructure under-investments of the Spanish government in Catalonia. The idea that the Spanish government's fiscal and economic policies had a negative impact that probably amplified the effects of the crisis in Catalonia became relatively widespread.

However, under closer scrutiny, the empirical facts do not support the idea that the crisis was the primary or key driver of the movement. There are at least two reasons. First, because once the crisis ended around 2014 and both Spain and Catalonia recovered the path of economic growth, the movement did not fade away as one would have expected if the crisis were its driving force. On the contrary, the movement intensified, organised the referendum in October 2017 and reached its record-high number of absolute votes at the December 2017 Catalan elections, with 2.1 million. Second, there is no correlation at the local level between the growth of the pro-independence vote and increases in unemployment.

A second explanation, very widespread in Spain, attributes the surge in support for independence to nationalistic indoctrination through the Catalan schooling system. However, the empirical evidence does not support this idea either. The shift towards independence support was not the result of generational replacement, but happened in a relatively homogeneous way across generations. The magnitude, speed and generational composition of the shift is not compatible with the idea of school indoctrination. Indeed, there is no clear empirical relationship between age and independence support, except those over 65 – the only group in which those with pro-union views consistently outnumber pro-independence supporters by about 8 percentage points.

There are also reasons to think that the surge was not primarily driven by changes in national identity, as suggested by the indoctrination hypothesis. National identification is usually measured in Catalonia through a scale in which respondents express their self-identification as 'Only Catalan', 'more Catalan than Spanish', 'More Spanish' or 'Only Spanish'. The proportion of those with exclusive Catalan identities was relatively stable around 20 per cent, and increased up to 30 per cent in an abrupt way by the end of 2012. This was not a progressive change that preceded the surge in support for independence, but rather a quick increase that, if anything, followed the shifts in constitutional preferences. Moreover, the share of those that support independence is consistently over 10 percentage points higher than those that self-identify as only Catalans.

Therefore, we can regard the surge in independence support among Catalan citizens as a reaction to the political context. The perception that further autonomy was not possible within Spain, and the trend towards recentralisation by Spanish central authorities led a large number of Catalan voters to shift towards demanding full independence.

After the realignment: 2013–7

Since 2013, support for independence at the polls has remained stable at around 47–48 per cent. This is the same level of support that pro-independence parties received in the 2015 and 2017 elections. Therefore, the realignment of 2010 to 2013 is over and we are now in a more stable position.

However, under the apparent stability, some important things have been changing. First, the increasing mobilisation has led to a slow but continued increase in the electoral support of pro-independence parties. In 2012, they got 1.6 million votes. In 2015, they reached 1.9 million and in 2017 the number had grown to 2.1 million.

This modest tendency has been neutralised by an increased mobilisation of the anti-independence voters. In 2017 the anti-independence groups organised their first mass demonstrations, and in the elections were able to mobilise 1.9 million voters.

The second trend is that positions in both camps seem to be increasingly entrenched. The electoral success of the extreme anti-independence party, Ciudadanos, seems to reveal an increasing polarisation of the pro-union camp.

In the pro-independence camp, there has also been some movement below the surface. An indicator of these changes is the fact that, while in 2010 over 35 per cent of those that favoured independence in a dichotomous question chose a federal arrangement as their preferred solution when given more options, in 2017 this number was a scarce 20 per cent.

Therefore, in the 2013 to 2017 period, despite the fact that the important realignment has ended, we have been witnessing some smaller changes towards an increase in support for independence but also a more intense mobilisation of the pro-union camp and a general trend towards more entrenched positions.

Who supports independence?

As might be expected, support for independence is not evenly spread across the Catalan population. If we look at the profile of those that support and oppose secession, some important differences do emerge. Using the most recent public opinion data available from the CEO (October 2017), we can explore these differences.

First, there is an important difference depending on the mother tongue, which is closely related to family origin in Catalonia. 82 per cent of those that have Catalan as their first language support independence, while only 28 per cent of those that spoke Spanish at home share this preference for secession. This points to an asymmetric divide, as the share of Catalan-speakers that oppose independence is significantly lower than the share of Spanish speakers that support it.

Despite the fact that language is one of the main predictors, there are other significant differences between the groups. Regarding age, the distribution of support is relatively similar across age groups with the notable exception of the oldest segment of the population. It is only among the over 65s that the anti-independence camp has a clear advantage of over 8 percentage points. Among the other groups, pro-independence supporters are a majority. This seems an important element to consider if one wants to forecast the future evolution of the political alignments in Catalonia.

Some differences also emerge if we look at other variables. Women are four percentage points less supportive of independence than men. This is mostly driven by the age effect, since women tend to outlive men, and they represent a larger share of the over 65s. Religious citizens are also less supportive of independence than the non-religious, among whom support for secession outnumbers opposition by almost 15 percentage points. People living in small villages and small towns tend to be more supportive of independence, while those living in middle-sized cities (between 50,000 and 250,000 inhabitants) are less so. These are the areas were the bulk of the migrants from southern Spain settled between the 1950s and the 1970s. In Barcelona, on the contrary, the two groups are even.

Left-right self-identification is also related to support for independence. Those on the far-left and left of the spectrum are overwhelmingly pro-independence, 67 and 57 per cent respectively, while those at the centre and right are predominantly pro-union. In some sense, the traditional identification of Spanish nationalism with the right contributes in this alignment between left-right identification and preferences regarding secession. The direction of the causality, thus, is not clear. It might be that some people self-identify as left or right because they support or oppose independence, and not the other way around.

Who is leading? The role of parties and social movements

While arguably the key driver of the realignment was the popular dissatisfaction with Spanish institutions, Catalan political actors did play a role. Preference realignments are usually not just a mechanical reaction to the evolving political context, and this case is no exception. It is perhaps more accurate to portray it as the combined effect of the evolution explained above and the successful mobilisation strategy put forward by pro-independence political parties and grassroots movements, that have had a central role in the process.

Even if a pro-independence movement has always been present in Catalonia, it started to gain traction around 2006, with the first large demonstration protesting amendments by Spanish Congress to the proposed statute reform passed by the Catalan Parliament in 2005. That demonstration was not called on an explicitly pro-independence stance, but it quickly became clear that the mobilisation had taken this character. In 2007, a protest against poor service in the Catalan commuter train network, which had suffered systematic underinvestment by its Spanish government management, also turned into an openly pro-independence march.

More importantly, in 2009 in a small town north of Barcelona, Arenys de Munt, the local council together with some local community groups decided to organise an unofficial referendum on independence. The public opposition of the Spanish government, which tried to forbid it, and of some Spanish far-right groups, which threatened to crack down on the participants, gave considerable notoriety to an event that might have passed unnoticed otherwise. A large pro-independence mobilisation in Arenys de Munt then spurred a snowball process of referenda across the country. By 2011, over half of the Catalan municipalities, including Barcelona, had held their own consultations. And, even if they were unofficially organised by volunteers and local groups, and turnout was on average below 30 per cent, they became crucial in strengthening of the pro-independence grassroots movement.

In 2011, an important part of the myriad of local groups that had taken part in their organisation as well as many of those that had been explicitly created to organise them, joined forces in a new mass grassroots movement called Assemblea Nacional Catalana (ANC). The ANC today has tens of thousands of members, and a large number of local and sectorial branches. Its first President Carme Forcadell, who became the speaker of the Catalan Parliament in September 2015, and her successor, Jordi Sánchez, are now in prison, sentenced to nine years for their role in the independence referendum.

Together with the ANC, a cultural organisation called Òmnium Cultural, which had been founded during the Francoist dictatorship to protect the Catalan language and culture, took an increasingly political stance, experiencing a great increase in membership. Òmnium's President, Jordi Cuixart, is another of the political prisoners. On the days following of his testimony at the Supreme Court in March 2019 membership reached over 160,000. Both groups have organised what are arguably the largest demonstrations in contemporary Catalonia. Every year since 2012, on 11 September pro-independence marches have reached turnout figures of between 800,000 and 1 million participants to commemorate the Catalans' national day.

These large demonstrations are only the most visible part of a dense and increasingly well-organised grassroots movement that has been extremely active during the whole period. In some way, this can be seen as one of the key defining features of the pro-independence movement. A dense network of organisations, volunteers and participants has been forged between 2009 and 2017. The pro-independence parties got about 2.1 million votes, and the pro-independence demonstrations gathered crowds of over 1 million. Therefore, the ratio of demonstrators per voter, of about 0.5, is remarkably high.

All the marches and activities of the movement had had a peaceful and festive character. This had led some observers to question the degree of commitment of its participants. However, the fact that on 1 October 2017 2.3 million people participated in the referendum despite the violent crackdown by the Spanish police probably means that the mobilisation is not only wide but also intense. This indicates that a substantial part of the Catalan electorate (43 per cent) was willing to take personal risks in order to pursue the independence path.

More generally, the centrality of such grassroots movements and the political mobilisation signal the importance of social capital as a crucial asset and mechanism of reproduction of the Catalan pro-independence movement. It has relied, not only on the explicitly pro-independence organisations, but also on a large number of non-political associations that in one way or another have given their support to the movement: from sport clubs to cultural and leisure associations.

This stands in contrast to the anti-independence groups, which have not been able to mobilise their followers with a similar level of intensity, despite several attempts. Often the most militant fringes, linked to the small Spanish nationalistic far-right groups, lead the pro-union street demonstrations. The 2017 march was an exception: the pro-union groups were finally able to organise some large-scale protests although not comparable in scale to those of the pro-independence movement.

Political parties, instability

The Catalan party system took shape during the first years of the democratic period and was stable over the years 1984 to 2010. During this period the number of parties and their relative share of electoral support experienced little change. The intense changes of political preferences experienced by the Catalan electorate during the last few years have conditioned the policy positions of the Catalan parties in the electoral arena. The Catalan political party system had been stable for over two decades. However, the surge of the pro-independence movements has upset this stability and is bound to give rise to a new party system.

The Catalan political debate has always had two dimensions: the usual left-right ideological dimension, and a dimension determined by the preferences for decentralisation. The ideological dimension, based on different preferences for economic and social policies is usually considered to represent the main, and often unique, issue of the political debates in many countries.

The decentralisation dimension is usually relevant in federations and especially in multi-national states. On this dimension, policy positions are defined according to the claims made by political parties on the allocation of decision power among the different levels of government.

Until the first decade of the 21st century the political preferences of Catalan society with regards to ideology covered a wide spectrum: from the extreme right to the extreme left. Nevertheless, the spread of political preferences with respect to decentralisation was rather moderate. There were indeed claims for different degrees of decentralisation, but, on the extremes, these claims were held by very small minorities of the population. Accordingly, the policy positions of the main political parties were moderate with respect to the decentralisation issue.

Up until 2010, the Catalan party system consisted of five parties. CiU was the centre-right coalition that had the largest electoral support during this period. The Catalan socialist party, PSC, had the second largest electoral support. Two other parties had smaller levels of electoral support, but played significant roles in the coalitions supporting the different governments of this period: PP was the main Spanish rightist party, and ERC was a Catalan left party with claims of a long-run wish for full independence. Finally, Iniciativa per Catalunya-Verds-Esquerra Unida i Alternativa (ICV-EUiA) was a leftist coalition of green and former communist parties.

Given the size of the parties, majority coalitions could involve all kinds of cross ideological agreements among parties on both issues. However, during the period 1990 to 2010 all the parliamentary majorities were defined by coalitions based on the parties' affinity to the ideology dimension. There were two kinds of governments, those of CiU with support of PP, or a left coalition government formed by PSC with ICV-EUiA and ERC. The salience of the decentralisation issue was clearly outweighed by the salience of the ideology issue.

With the surge of grassroots movements for independence and the switch of electoral preferences towards independence, the stability exhibited by the Catalan party system for over 20 years is now long passed. Catalan society's political preferences have changed, and polls show a wide support for full independence. Up until 2012, the preferences of the voters on the decentralisation issue were moderate, concentrating on the middle range of the decentralisation dimension. These preferences have now spread along the extremes of the decentralisation dimension in a way that has mostly abandoned moderate positions and concentrated most of their weight on the extreme of full decentralisation, that is, the creation of a separate state. In addition, the strength and massive character displayed by pro-independence popular movements reveal that the intensity of voters' preferences for extreme policy positions on the decentralisation issue might have also increased. Thus, the relative prominence of the two dimensions has changed dramatically with the decentralisation dimension becoming much more salient over time, as well as more polarised. The radicalisation of the voters over this issue has produced an increase of the voter turnout over this period.

At the same time as the electorate was shifting its preferences on decentralisation, three new parties entered the Catalan political area. Ciudadanos is a Catalan party that claimed an ambiguous position on the ideology dimension, but very extreme Spanish nationalism. The origin of this party may be explained as a response to the increasingly intense preference for extreme centralisation among some voters that was not immediately matched by the existing centralist parties' platforms. CUP is a Catalan party that was born at the municipal level and holds strong preferences in favour of both full independence and extreme leftist ideology. Finally, the latest entrant, Podemos, is a Spanish leftist party that has broken into the political arena with great success since the 2014 European elections, and in Catalonia they have run in coalitions with ICV, advocating for more decentralisation than the status quo, but not independence.

The strength of the pro-independence claims expressed by relentlessly massive demonstrations, the consistent support for independence at the public opinion polls, and the entry of new parties in the Catalan political arena faced the established parties with a new electoral scenario. Their policy positions had comfortably remained unchanged for over two decades, but the new scenario forced them to tune in their positions to remain competitive under the drastic changes in the electorate's preferences and the challenge of new entrants.

How did traditional parties adapt? On the one hand, the PP and ERC could adapt in a very easy and natural way. The PP moved slightly its position from moderate to more extreme centralisation claims, in order to defend its constituency from the competition of the clearly pro-centralisation C's. ERC moved its position from moderate claims of decentralisation with a long-term wish for independence to an explicit claim for full independence. This was an easy adjustment since this party's historical platform had always expressed wishes for full independence. The strategy chosen by ICV has been to hold a leftist position on the ideology dimension forming electoral coalition with Podemos, and remain ambiguous on the decentralisation issue.

The need to adapt had more dramatic consequences for the two larger parties. PSC suffered severe internal turmoil. Tensions tore the party apart. Several small factions broke away to set up new small parties with pro-independence positions, and the larger faction took a centralist position. As a result, the PSC suffered a drastic decrease in electoral support. CiU first addressed its internal tensions by having two of its leaders to deliver two different messages. This strategy of contradictory platforms was facilitated because CiU was in fact a long-lasting coalition of two different parties: Convergència Democràtica de Catalunya and Unió Democràtica de Catalunya. The strain of these contradictory approaches broke up the coalition in the summer of 2015.

President Artur Mas lead the transition of his party, CDC, adapting its electoral platform to support independence. He organised the informal popular consultation on independence in November 2014, and later on pushed for an electoral coalition with ERC and independents, Junts pel Sí, who ran on an unambiguous independence platform and won the Catalan Parliament election in September 2015. The coalition won, but as the condition to obtain the support of CUP, Mas had to step out as President to be replaced by Carles Puigdemont. Puigdemont's coalition cabinet then took office with a mandate for independence that led to the self-determination referendum of 1 October, 2017.

Impossible compromise

Massive grassroots movements, together with opinion polling evidence showing an increase preference for independence and the overall political climate, presented clear demands directed to the political leaders waiting for a governmental response. Both the Spanish and Catalan governments and political parties were forced to react. In particular, the Presidents of the Catalan and Spanish governments faced an inescapable challenge.

The Catalan Presidents, first President Mas and later on President Puigdemont, wanted to satisfy a sustained demand of a large part of the Catalan society to hold a referendum on the independence issue. On the other hand, President Rajoy positioned himself against responding to the demands for independence in any way. For a long time, he even denied the existence of a political problem in Catalonia. These divergent reactions left little room for compromise. They were, however, fully consistent with rational political calculus given the circumstances.

First of all, as the Catalan population amounts only to 15.7 per cent of the Spanish total population, the country contributes only a fraction of the Spanish electorate. Furthermore, the support that President Rajoy's party, the Spanish conservative party PP, had received historically from Catalonia has on average been below 20 per cent. Thus, even if a good share of the Catalan constituency decided to punish President Rajoy for not satisfying their demands, the effect this would have on his nationwide electoral chances would not be dramatic. Furthermore, the share of the Catalan electorate that has remained loyal to President Rajoy's party does certainly not coincide with the electorate that supports independence. Therefore, even if a large part of the Catalan electorate supports independence, the Popular Party has so far rightly assumed that their lack of response to these demands does not hurt their electoral chances. Hence, President Rajoy had no electoral incentive to satisfy the popular demand. In addition, President Rajoy's ideology on the issue, based on the indivisibility of Spain, together with his need to satisfy his expected electoral support from the rest of Spain could have been jeopardised if he had to show any ideological weakness in this respect. Thus, his decision not to act upon the popular demand for independence, even ignoring it, was clearly a rational action on his part.

On the other hand, the electoral support for the Catalan Presidents relied only on the Catalan constituency. Therefore, the effect of possible voters' retaliation could seriously undermine their support. And most of their electoral support coincided with the large proportion of the society that had demonstrated in favour of an independent Catalan state. Therefore, to maintain the support of this electorate, they were required to respond to the popular demands. Their inaction was bound to imply large electoral loses.

Since the optimal strategies for the Catalan and Spanish governments were completely opposed, it is not surprising that they could not find a common solution to the demand of the Catalan society. This was the origin of the conflict of interest that made any possible agreement impossible. The electoral incentives that they faced were simply incompatible. While on the one hand these incentives led Catalan Presidents to offer full support to the demands for independence, at the same time, the Spanish government's incentives led them to ignore and dismiss it.

Bibliographical note:

The evolution of public support for Independence in Catalonia has been previously discussed by a number of academic works. In Muñoz, J, and Tormos, R, 'Economic expectations and support for secession in Catalonia: between causality and rationalisation', *European Political Science Review*, 7 2, 2015. Rodon, T and Guinjoan, M, 'When the context matters: Identity, secession and the spatial dimension in Catalonia', *Political Geography*, 2018 discuss the contextual factors, and Hierro, M J, and Gallego, A 'Identities in between: Political conflict and ethnonational identities in multicultural states', *Journal of Conflict Resolution*, 62 6, 2018, presents evidence on the process of polarisation. See also: Aragones, E and Ponsati, C, 'Negotiations and political strategies in the contest for Catalan independence', in *Catalonia: a New Independent state in Europe?* edited by X. Cuadras-Morató, Abingdon, 2016. Culla, J B, *El tsunami. Com i per què el sistema de partits català ha esdevingut irreconeixible* Barcelona, 2017, analyses the Catalan party system.

Chapter 5

The economic costs and benefits of Independence

Although the creation of a new state is essentially a political decision, it is one that might have very substantial economic consequences that ought to be analysed in detail. In fact, some of the economic implications of independence are so important that they inevitably occupy a central place in some of the most significant disputes between its advocates and opponents. Moreover, these questions have been shown to be a key determinant of the popular support for or against secession. This was clearly the case in Québec and Scotland during their respective independence referendums, and it is also the case in all the current debates about the prospect of an independent Catalan state. This chapter will be focused on the appraisal of the main economic consequences of the eventual establishment of Catalonia as a new independent state. In order to do this, we will identify and analyse the main opportunities and threats that, in the long run, the Catalan economy would face in the new constitutional situation as well as the economic risks derived from a transition process to the new status that is likely to be rather complicated.

An independent Catalonia would be geographically smaller than most of the countries of the current European Union (EU). Its territory of a little more than 32,000 square kilometres, which corresponds to only 6.3 per cent of Spain as a whole, makes it slightly larger than Belgium. On the other hand, it contains a much greater share of Spain's population, at 16.2 per cent. In absolute terms, this amounts to 7.5 million people, a little above the population of Bulgaria and not far away from the median value of all the countries in the EU, where as many as 13 states have fewer inhabitants.

Catalonia is economically the most important region of Spain, accounting for 20.1 per cent of total gross domestic product (GDP). It has a diversified economic structure and is relatively open to trade and investment. According to its economic size (measured as GDP at current market prices) in 2015, Catalonia would occupy the 14th position in a hypothetical EU29 ranking, just below Finland. It is also a relatively rich region, so that the level of GDP per capita is substantially higher (19.3 per cent) than the Spanish average. It is also relatively wealthy within the EU. Its GDP per capita is 10 per cent higher than average, placing the region between the United Kingdom and France.

If Catalonia were to become an independent state, Catalan citizens would go from being part of a country of more than 46 million people to belonging to a much smaller state. Would this affect their economic prospects? Modern research in economics has failed to find any convincing evidence of the *bigger is better* hypothesis, that is, the existence of a positive relationship between size (generally approximated by population) and the economic performance of countries. More casual evidence coming from looking at a myriad of international rankings (on competitiveness, development, happiness and so on), where one can find small countries systematically occupying some of the top spots, seem to confirm the idea that size is not a determinant factor of economic success. From this perspective, secession should not affect the economic prospects of Catalonia in a significant way.

As a matter of fact, economists and other social scientists have been paying attention for some time to the issue of the evolution of the number and size of nations in the world. It is well documented that the last 70 years have witnessed an increase in the number of countries to a record high of more than 190, and the consequent decrease of their average relative size. That is, today there are many more countries and they are much smaller than in 1945. At the same time, there has been a proliferation of international treaties and organisations fostering trade and economic cooperation and integration – for example, the European Union. To explain these facts, modern economic theory emphasizes the effects of, first, economic globalisation and, second, the reduction of military means as the way of resolving conflicts among nations.[1] Big states may no longer be optimal political structures when some of their main benefits (access to larger markets and more effective defence of national interests in case of international conflict) can be achieved through membership of international institutions. Depending on factors such as the existence of idiosyncratic national preferences for public goods and economies of scale in their production, the new optimal political organisation of the world is likely to be a two-level government structure. In the first level, smaller countries would optimally provide public welfare services such as health care and education and income redistribution programmes. In the second level, multinational institutions like the EU would be in charge of other traditional government functions such as market regulation and competition and monetary policies. Somewhat paradoxically, according to this view it is the greater degree of international integration implied by the increasing globalisation of trade and more intense political cooperation among states that is behind the growing levels of political fragmentation reflected in the rising number of countries in the world.

Few doubt that Catalonia has the economic potential to continue being a prosperous country in the European context. After all, it has a diversified and relatively modern economy. It is commercially open to the world and its capital, Barcelona, is consistently ranked as one of the most attractive cities in Europe. The Catalan economy benefits from the presence of foreign capital in numerous sectors, such as transport equipment, chemicals, pharmaceuticals, food processing, ICT and logistics. It also has some of the best universities and research centres in Spain. From a long term perspective, an independent Catalonia could end up being just another small and relatively rich European country whose economic success would depend on the factors that determine the competitiveness of countries (among others, quality of institutions and economic policies, social cohesion, education and human capital, physical infrastructures, openness to trade and promotion of market competition and innovation). However, things might not look so rosy once one takes a short-term perspective. There are a number of important transitional issues that will have to be addressed during the process of independence and might imply sizeable costs for Catalan citizens and companies. This might make secession a more traumatic prospect for many of them.

These transition costs might crucially depend on the degree of cooperation between the continuing and the seceding state during the separation process. In the case

5

of Catalonia, which is today part of the EU and the Economic and Monetary Union (EMU), it is also very important to keep in view the actions and attitudes of the different member states and EU institutions with regards to the secession process. All this makes transition costs uncertain and highly contingent on the strategic interaction of the different political agents, both at domestic and international levels. For instance, the Catalan pro-independence supporters are clearly interested in reaching an agreement with the Spanish authorities on a democratic procedure to settle the matter (e.g. an accorded referendum) and a posterior good faith negotiation over the terms of the secession. This would help clarify the transition period and reduce uncertainty over fundamental issues during the independence process. But, for this same reason, the Spanish government and its allies have all the incentives not to submit to such an agreement, making the transition process as difficult as possible and increasing its potential costs, thus reducing the popular support for independence.

The biggest economic opportunities for an independent Catalonia would be a direct consequence of its greater political power. Full control of fiscal resources and autonomous economic policies are the main opportunities arising from independence. From a medium and long-term perspective, they could allow for stronger economic growth and better welfare prospects for Catalonia. Taking into account the relationship between some of the main economic growth factors (infrastructures, education, research and development) and the level of public expenditures, it is not far-fetched to say that independence could increase not only the disposable income of Catalan citizens, but also their economic growth prospects in the medium term. Of course, this outcome should not be taken for granted for several reasons, especially during a complicated transition period. First, the new state would be very indebted in the first years and this would greatly condition its fiscal policies. Second, it would need, from the very beginning, solid public institutions and honest and competent politicians to manage economic policy efficiently.

Greater political power means better economic opportunities

The current system of inter-regional allocation of taxes and spending in Spain would minimise the fiscal risks arising from independence, since this would immediately put an end to the annual negative net fiscal flows going from Catalonia to the rest of Spain. It would also ensure that the Catalan state collected more than enough fiscal revenues to finance all public services currently enjoyed by its citizens. From the analysis of the period of 2002 to 2014, the Catalan fiscal imbalance – that is, the difference between all central government expenditures which are allocated to Catalonia minus all taxes collected by the central government in Catalonia – has been estimated by the Catalan government to be between 6 and 8.3 per cent of Catalan GDP on average every year. The Spanish government also published some estimates of the territorial fiscal flows for all the regions in Spain. There are several methodological differences with the estimations of the Catalan government and, consequently, they are not directly comparable. For the record, the figures published by the Spanish government systematically correspond to around 80 per cent of the value of the estimations by the Catalan government (for the years 2011, 2012 and 2013, for which the figures are available from both sources). The exact figure depends on the calculation method used in the estimation. Thus, even though the new Catalan state would probably start its life heavily indebted (mainly because the Spanish state is currently bearing high levels of public debt and this would predictably be split between the two new countries), and this would undoubtedly restrict its fiscal policies, the reversion of the secular fiscal imbalance with the Spanish central government would provide the country with a clear opportunity to start building its fiscal credibility and guarantee the sustainability of its public finances. As a matter of fact, since Catalonia is richer and has a lower unemployment rate than Spain and, after independence, would enjoy a better fiscal outlook too, it is likely to enjoy a better credit rating and, thus, a lower risk premium.

Supporters of independence also argue that public policies designed and implemented by the Spanish central government very often are not optimal from the point of view of the Catalan economy and its specificities, among which the larger weight of the industrial, tourism and export sectors and the smaller weight of the public sector are often mentioned. Thus, there would be additional potential gains from independence due to improvements in economic policy, relying on the fact that Catalan authorities would be able to implement differentiated policy measures, better tailored to satisfy the needs and preferences of Catalan firms and citizens. In other words, while in principle it is not reasonable to expect that Catalan policy makers would be more, or less, competent than their Spanish counterparts, it is likely that their policy measures, addressed to a different constituency, are different and more efficient. Admittedly, the potential benefits of autonomous decision making under independence, while clear from the conceptual point of view, are very difficult to appraise quantitatively in a rigorous manner.

Notwithstanding this, there is a particular field in which the inadequacies of centralised public policy have been particularly felt by the Catalan productive sectors: the provision and management of public infrastructures, in particular transport (i.e. roads, airports, ports and railways). There is a general consensus in Catalan society, including most political parties, business associations and trade unions that the lack of a well-managed network of transport infrastructure adapted to the specific needs of Catalan firms and citizens, for which the centralist policies of the Spanish government are mainly to blame, have been seriously detrimental to the competitiveness of the Catalan economy. This has hindered general mobility in the metropolitan area of Barcelona, export activities of Catalan firms, and the attraction of foreign investment into the region. In the context of the very old economic and political rivalry between Barcelona and Madrid, a very centralised railway network and an airport policy designed to favour the interests of the Spanish capital are, from the point of view of many Catalan citizens, two additional proofs that too often they are not getting a fair deal out of the Spanish government policies.

The costs of political disintegration

A decline in economic exchanges between Catalonia and Spain is considered one potential negative economic consequence of independence. Although this might affect different types of economic relationships, labour and capital market flows for instance, it is trade flows of goods and services that have received most of the attention of the analysts. The potential for disruption in trade relations between Catalonia and Spain, and perhaps other European countries, seems to many observers one of the foremost threats to the Catalan economy in the eventual case of secession. Despite the accelerated process of internationalisation that the Catalan economy has experienced, especially since the mid-1980s, the Spanish market remains important for many exporting companies in the region. Opponents of secession often refer to this situation to make their case about the undesirability of the separation of Catalonia from Spain, at least from an economic point of view. According to their argument, independence would affect this important commercial relationship and reduce the volume of exports of domestic firms to the Spanish market. This would represent a very large economic cost for the Catalan economy, offsetting the potential benefits derived from the creation of a new state. In 2017, the Spanish market still absorbed 35.5 per cent of Catalonia's total exports. The rest of markets were far behind. France (10.2 per cent), Germany (7.2 per cent) and Italy (5.7 per cent) were the largest destinations for Catalan exports after Spain. Nevertheless, there has been a definite downward trend in the relative importance of the

Spanish market. In 20 years, this has almost halved, going from 63.5 per cent in 1995 to the current value.

Although there are not studies specifically analysing this issue, it is likely that, at least in part, the recent trend showing growing support for independence among Catalan citizens, including important parts of the business community, is linked to underlying structural economic changes that point to a reduction of the dependence of the Catalan economy on exports to the Spanish market. As a matter of fact, some of the most vocal opponents to the independence political project within the business community can be associated with 'captive' sectors that either maintain Spain as one of their most important markets or crucially depend on Spanish government regulations – this would be the case of banking, insurance or public utilities, for example. In contrast, firms catering mainly for the domestic Catalan market and truly global exporters facing the world economy are more likely to make a more favourable appraisal of the net gains of secession, if only because they are less exposed to its long-run costs.

Measuring the potential changes in trade with Spain as a result of secession is not an easy exercise. Comerford and Rodríguez-Mora (2014) make a daring attempt.[2] Departing from the well-known observation that regional economies within a country are more commercially integrated than countries with each other, the so-called 'border effect' in international trade, they hypothesise that an independent Catalonia would end up as commercially integrated with Spain as Portugal is – Portugal being Spain's closest trade partner. Under this assumption, they estimate a sizeable reduction of trade flows between the two territories, causing a 9.5 per cent fall in Catalonia's GDP. It is very important to bear in mind that this would not be an immediate outcome of the independence process. A similar study by the British government for the case of Scotland before the referendum in 2014 predicted that the trade effects due to the creation of a Scottish state would cause a decrease of 4 per cent of GDP after 30 years of independence, which amounts to an average annual loss of 0.13 per cent. Also considering 30 years as the relevant period for the Catalan case would represent an average annual fall in GDP of 0.32 per cent, still small when compared with the potential fiscal gains arising from independence. Nevertheless, and regarding the question of whether 30 years is the relevant period for the analysis, one should also take into account that trade links might be far more durable. An example of this is that in 1971, almost 50 years after independence in 1922, Ireland was still sending 66 per cent of its total exports to the United Kingdom. Finally, these authors fail to take into account in their exercise that independence, while enhancing the effect of some factors that contribute to the increase of trading frictions between Catalonia and Spain, may simultaneously decrease trading frictions between Catalonia and other countries. A good example of this could be transport infrastructure investments. It might be that the new Catalan state sets its priorities trying to improve the now neglected connections with Europe. This could make the border effect with Spain larger and, thus, reduce trade but, at the same time, it might also improve the commercial relationship with France and other European countries.

An uncertain transition process

Independence is a very complex and risky operation from an economic and political point of view. It implies a break from the status quo and a radical shift in the institutional set-up of the country. In the context of a liberal democracy, it also requires majoritarian popular political support. Hence, the particular characteristics of the transition process towards the new state become key elements of the political calculus of both the pro-independence and pro-union camps. Those supporting independence are interested in having a smooth as possible transition to independence, in which there is agreement among the different parties about a democratic procedure to reach a decision and the need for good faith negotiations over the terms of the split between the two countries. This would have the advantage of reassuring citizens about the political and economic viability of the new state and reducing their levels of uncertainty about the future political status of the country. Lack of dialogue and, needless to say, agreement on these matters, arguably the preferred strategy of the Spanish government and pro-union parties, creates a great deal of uncertainty and makes independence a riskier political undertaking, deeming it less palatable for large sectors of society who could fear it on the basis of its mostly unknown, but potentially large, costs.

Of course, there is a very radical difference between a negotiated and a non-negotiated secession process.

While the latter case implies large costs for all parties involved, the former opens the possibility of drastically reducing them to a minimum and, with it, reaching political compromises. Under a good faith negotiation, necessarily with the mediation of a third party, Catalans could agree to maintain transfers to Spain for a number of years or assume a relatively large share of public debt after independence.

At any rate, the present lack of consensus means that the level of uncertainty on some fundamental questions affecting the Catalan economy is likely to stay high. It is worth mentioning a few of them. First, the circumstances of recognition by the international community are unclear, with the potential ambiguities about the legal status of Catalan citizens and firms. Second, doubts will arise about membership of EU and EMU, which have obvious trade and financial implications for many firms and the banking and financial sectors of the Catalan economy. Finally, fears about episodes of civil unrest and police interventions might be difficult to dispel.

In particular, doubts about the legal status of firms and membership of EU and EMU might influence the location decisions of companies. Also, fears about political turmoil and civil unrest might frighten away visitors and harm the tourism sector. In general, greater uncertainty might slow investment decisions of firms and diminish the confidence levels of consumers. All these circumstances might result in lower rates of economic growth. In the context of the current political confrontation between the pro-independence and pro-union camps, the issue has been the object of a fierce rhetorical battle between both sides about the actual size of the threat to the Catalan economy. While the pro-independence camp tends to minimise the negative economic effects of the political process and blame them on the lack of political negotiations between the parties, the pro-union side argues that the Catalan economy is already badly suffering due to the political stalemate created and that the Catalan government is the main culprit of the situation for its insistence on pursuing political objectives contrary to the Spanish Constitution.

Despite some dismal forecasts by the Spanish government and other observers, it is fair to say that the consequences of the political conflict on the Catalan and Spanish economies were negligible until the last quarter of 2017. After the referendum on 1 October, things got a lot more complicated. Images of Spanish police brutality went viral all over the world, scaring away some visitors and causing complaints by representatives of the tourism industry about a decline in the number of reservations. Uncertainty about the legal status of Catalan firms, consumer boycott campaigns against their products and even some degree of unsubtle pressure exerted by the Spanish government induced more than 3,000 Catalan companies to initiate the procedures to move their legal domicile elsewhere in Spain. Among them, there were the two biggest Catalan banks and some of the main firms in different sectors such as insurance or public utilities. In many cases this was done under the auspices of the Spanish government, who exerted pressure and made the shifting easier by approving a decree that removed a previous requirement for a shareholders' meeting to grant permission first.

In the case of the banks, it has been reported that this change took place under the added pressure of massive deposit withdrawals by public institutions controlled by the Spanish government.

After a few weeks of intense political drama in Catalonia, it was hard to maintain the stance that the situation did not have negative economic implications. Nevertheless, catastrophic forecasts of chaos and rapid economic decline proved to be completely inaccurate. A more balanced view of the matter would have to first acknowledge the resilience of the Catalan economy, which was able to cope rather effectively with the political shock. At the same time, however, all political agents should be aware of the potential economic dangers of a disordered transition period. Since the growing perception of these economic risks is one of the factors that could weaken support for independence in the immediate future, this concern should be especially relevant to pro-independence strategists.

To conclude, despite all the fuss about the harm the political process was inflicting on the economy, the short-term damage suffered by Catalonia at the aggregate level at the end of 2017 and the beginning of 2018 was insignificant (Table 1). In fact, economic and employment growth still kept a stronger pace in Catalonia than in Spain and the EU. It is certainly too early to tell at this stage, but the real dangers now are that the political situation in Catalonia remains in a deadlock and the levels of uncertainty are not reduced, affecting the prospects of the economy in the near future in a more serious way.

	2016	2017	2017 Q3	2017 Q4	2018 Q1	2018 Q2	2018
CAT	3.4	3.3	3.5	3.8	3.3	2.8	2.6
ESP	3.2	3.0	2.9	3.1	2.8	2.5	2.5
EU	2.0	2.4	2.8	2.7	2.4	2.2	1.9

GDP. Year-over-year growth rates

	2016	2017	2017 Q3	2017 Q4	2018 Q1	2018 Q2	2018
CAT	3.4	2.9	2.9	3.5	3.3	2.7	2.7
ESP	2.7	2.6	2.8	2.6	2.4	2.8	2.7
EU	1.5	1.4	1.5	1.4	1.4	1.0	–

Employment. Year-over-year growth rates

Table 1

Sources: Idescat and Eurostat

Concluding remarks

Catalonia, like most European countries, has important economic policy challenges in the years ahead. These are related to reforms that are necessary to construct a more prosperous and resilient economy and a more cohesive society. Although the political debate today in Catalonia is mainly focused on the need to separate from Spain, it should be clear that there is a connection between this and the aforementioned challenges.

According to data released by the European Commission in 2016, Catalonia was the fourth richest of Spain's 17 regions, but only the 12th region in terms of the Social Progress Index (SPI), an aggregate index of 50 social and environmental indicators that capture several dimensions of social progress. This is the kind of shocking result that might help understanding the support for Catalan independence. Many citizens and voters in Catalonia have reached the conclusion that they are getting a bad deal out of the economic and social policies of successive Spanish governments. To give an example, public expenditure in education in Catalonia was in 2015 a meagre 3.15 per cent of GDP, much lower than the corresponding figure in Spain of 4.39 per cent, which is already modest by European standards. For those citizens, the economic and political debate in which the Catalan society is now immersed is above all about who controls fiscal resources and designs and implements effective public policies to build a more competitive and cohesive country.

Bibliographical note:

There are very few English written or translated books that take on the specific subject of the Catalan economy and the independence process. Good summaries can be found in Cuadras-Morató, X, *Catalonia: A New Independent State in Europe*, Abingdon, 2016 (chapter 6 is entirely devoted to analyse the issue) and in a collective volume edited by the Col·legi d'Economistes de Catalunya, *The Economy of* Catalonia (Questions and answers on the economic impact of independence), Barcelona, 2014. A shorter review can be found in a paper published by Antoni Castells, 'Catalonia and Spain at the Crossroads: Financial and Economic Aspects' *Oxford Review of Economic Policy*, 30, 2014. On the problem of transport infrastructure policy in Spain there is the book by Bel, G, *Infrastructure and the Political Economy of Nation Building in Spain (1720–2010)*, Eastbourne, 2012. The question of the fiscal flows between Catalonia and the Spanish Government has been dealt with in Bosch, N, Espasa, M and Solé-Oller, A (eds.) *The Political Economy of*

Inter-Regional Fiscal Flows, Cheltenham, 2010, and also Bel, G, *Disdain, Distrust and Dissolution (The Surge of Support for Independence in Catalonia)*, Eastbourne, 2015. On this, the interested reader can look at the data and analysis by the Catalan (http://economia.gencat.cat/ca/ambits-actuacio/analisi-finances-publiques/balanca-fiscal-catalunya-administracio-central/) and Spanish (http://www.hacienda.gob.es/es-ES/CDI/Paginas/OtraInformacionEconomica/Sistema-cuentas-territorializadas.aspx) governments. A group of Catalan economists and social scientists (under the collective name of Col·lectiu Wilson) have published very insightful analysis of all these issues in the web-page www.wilson.cat. On the economic analysis of the number of nations and the political structure of the world the reader could see the seminal work by Alesina, A and Spolaore, E, *The Size of Nations*, Cambridge Massachusetts, 2003, and a more modern paper by Gancia, G, Ponzetto, G and Ventura, J, Globalization and Political Structure, published as BGSE Working Paper n.878 2017.

5

Chapter 6

Catalonia and the right of self-determination

As World War One was drawing to an end, US President Woodrow Wilson stated in his February 1918 intervention to the American Congress on the causes and political consequences of the European conflagration, that 'national aspirations must be respected; people may now be dominated and governed only by their own consent'. Knocking down the international consensus on the inviolability of state sovereignty that had prevailed for several centuries, he then added that 'self-determination is not a mere phrase. It is an imperative principle of actions which statesmen will henceforth ignore at their peril'. Less than 30 years later, that general principle of self-determination was formally recognised as part of the international legal order after the United Nations voted, in its foundational Charter, to include, as one of its main purposes, 'to develop friendly relations among nations based on respect for the principle of equal rights and self-determination of peoples' (UN Charter, article 1.2).

Now, what are the foundations and limits of the right to self-determination? May the Catalan people appeal to it legitimately? May Catalonia exercise it without constraints or should it fulfil certain specific conditions? In this chapter, we respond to these questions in four steps. First, we describe the evolution of the international law and doctrine on self-determination – showing that the principle of self-determination has been formalised in a direct and explicit manner for its application in territories under colonial administration. Second, we argue that, even when it is not explicitly formalised, the right of self-determination has been deemed permissible in all other cases, provided that those who exercise it comply with two key conditions:

6

namely the principle *uti possidetis* and the absence of illicit violence. Third, we move beyond the analysis of the legality of the right of self-determination to summarise the main normative justifications that the current jurisprudence and philosophical debates seem to require its legitimate use and we connect them to the Catalan crisis. Finally, we suggest that, although Catalonia can appeal to the right to self-determination on legal grounds and for legitimate reasons, all parties (including European institutions) to the Catalan case may benefit from understanding it as an instance of 'internal enlargement' within the European Union.

The formalisation of the Right of Self-Determination in International Law

Although the principle of self-determination has its source of inspiration in the declaration of independence of the United States in 1776, the processes of separation of the Spanish colonies in Latin America and, in Europe, the national revolutions of 1848, it was only President Wilson's doctrine and the victory of the Allied powers in 1918, and again in 1945, that introduced it in the international order, reshaping the latter for good.

Since the Peace of Westphalia of 1648, the recognition of the exclusive sovereignty of each state over its own territory, as well as its corollary, the prohibition of intervention in the internal affairs of a state by any other state or any supra-national organisation, became the paramount principles governing the international system and the relationships between its members. That legal and political solution extended to the whole area of state action the formula 'cuius regio, eius religio' (in each realm, the king's religion), introduced for the first time in the peace of Augsburg in 1555 and according to which every German prince had the right to impose his religious confession on his territory, with the goal of pacifying a continent devastated by religious wars. Such a solution implied granting a fully legal and legitimate status to all states irrespective of the nature and quality of their political institutions. As a result, it denied that any individual rights could have any international standing above state sovereignty. In other words, the principle of exclusive sovereignty formalised in Westphalia made the state the only actor with the capacity to define what was permissible or not within its borders. That included the right of national self-determination: therefore, its recognition depended on strictly internal constitutional norms. That, in turn, made any peaceful independence processes exceptional. Before World War One, only Norway became fully sovereign without resorting to violence.

The democratic principles affirmed in the American declaration of independence, and embraced by the 19th century liberal movement, ended up clashing with the principle of absolute state sovereignty. As President Wilson pointed out in his speech to the US Congress, World War One 'had its roots in the disregard of the rights of small nations and of nationalities which lacked the union and the force to make good their claim to determine their own allegiances and their own forms of political life'. The only solution was to enter

covenants... which will render such things impossible for the future; and those covenants must be backed by the united force of all the nations that love justice and are willing to maintain it at any cost.

In other words, the system of Westphalia, where peace had been maintained through a precarious balance of power among states endowed with absolute sovereignty within their own jurisdiction, had to give way to a system based on international regulations, supported by supranational institutions such as the League of Nations and, later on, the United Nations, capable of regulating, in accordance with principles of universal justice, the relations between nations and people of the world.

Following the Wilson declaration, the right to self-determination underwent a gradual process of juridi-fication until it became a fully regulated right within the international legal system. The Treaty of Versailles of 1919 introduced, in a partially arbitrary way, the use of plebi-scites in some European territories to determine state boundaries according to the opinion of their inhabitants. Nevertheless, it took 30 years to formally recognise the right of self-determination at the international level – once the violation of national borders by Nazi Germany and the Holocaust persuaded the international community about the need to develop a Charter of the United Nations that explicitly included a set of democratic principles and human rights that should govern the international order.

Developing the principle of self-determination as stated in its article 1, the United Nations Charter established in article 76(b), which was included in chapter XII on non-autonomous territories, the possibility of a

> progressive development [of trust territories] towards self-government or independence as may be appropriate to the particular circumstances of

each territory and its peoples and the freely expressed wishes of the peoples concerned, and as may be provided by the terms of each trusteeship agreement.

The ambiguity of the terms employed, with self-determination referred to as a 'principle' and not as a 'right' and with independence seen as a goal to be achieved progressively, reflected a political compromise between the Soviet Union, interested in supporting the revolutionary movements of the Third World, and the United States, ideationally committed to self-determination but allied with the old European colonial powers.

Eventually, the post-war process of decolonisation triggered the transformation of self-determination from a general principle into a legally recognised right. Several United Nations resolutions referred to the right to self-determination in the 1950s. Shortly afterwards, the 'Declaration on the Granting of Independence to Colonial Countries and Peoples', approved by the General Assembly of the United Nations in December 1960, stated that 'all peoples have the right to self-determination' and that 'by virtue of that right they freely determine their political status and freely pursue their economic, social and cultural development' (provision no. 2). The right to self-determination was limited by the concurrent recognition of the existence of an international principle of territorial integrity. More precisely, the Declaration warned that 'any attempt aimed at the partial or total disruption of the national unity and the territorial integrity of a country' was 'incompatible with the purposes and principles of the Charter of the United Nations' (provision no 6). The principle of territorial integrity, whose political purpose was the stabilisation of the African continent, referred to the application of the principle *uti possidetis*, in accordance with which external borders had to be maintained, even if they had been artificially created by a colonial metropolis. In other words, a process of self-determination could not lead to the formation of a new country based on the aggregation of parts of several original states. As indicated in a ruling of the International Court of Justice on the border dispute between Mali and Burkina Faso (1986 ICJ 554, December 22), the purpose of its application was to avoid fratricidal struggles caused by border changes as a result of the withdrawal of the administrator power. Still, even the recognition of the principle of territorial integrity may not be used to undermine the right of self-determination. As the report of the independent expert on the promotion of a democratic and equitable international order submitted in accordance with the UN Assembly resolution 68/175 states, 'the principle of territorial integrity no longer possesses a higher status in international law than the right of self-determination, which is anchored in the Charter of the United Nations and in the International Covenants on Human Rights. A balancing of rights and interests must be carried out, always with a view to achieving greater respect for human rights and widening the democratic space' (A/69/272, para. 82).

The permissibility of self-determination in non-colonial territories

The fact that the United Nations gradually refined the conditions under which the right of self-determination applied to colonial territories did not mean, however, that such a right did not exist in non-colonial regions. As recently stated by the International Court of Justice in its advisory opinion on Kosovo in 2010,

> State practice during this period points clearly to the conclusion that international law contained no prohibition of declarations of independence. During the second half of the 20th century, the international law of self-determination developed in such a way as to create a right to independence for the peoples of non-self-governing territories and peoples subject to alien subjugation, domination and exploitation.[1]

The Court's assertion was normative, that is, grounded on the principles of democracy and respect for human rights. Yet it was also empirical since, again according to the opinion on Kosovo, 'a great many new States have come into existence as a result of the exercise of this right' (ibid.). Bangladesh's independence from Pakistan in 1974, the division of Yugoslavia (and the recognition of its successor states by the international community) and the very doctrine developed by the Canadian Supreme Court on a possible secession of Québec show that the right of self-determination could and does take place in situations that are not strictly colonial.

Accepting that the sources of the right of self-determination are multiple, partly regulated directly by the United Nations (and clarified by the Court's own case law) and partly derived from the daily and flexible practice of the community of states, the International Court of Justice reminded all the consulting parties to the Kosovo question the fact that the Court could not confirm the existence of a right to self-determination beyond the one that the international community has already regulated (through the institutions that represent it) did not imply that it could not establish clearly that there is no international rule prohibiting the exercise of self-determination. In other words, the Court embraced a flexible and liberal interpretation of the modern legal order according to which anything that is not prohibited is permitted.

The right of self-determination should only remain limited by the exclusion of a process of separation based on 'an illicit resource of force or other serious violations of norms of international law' (section 81). As for the principle of territorial integrity, it continued to apply to the external borders of the original state. Hence, the Court could conclude that, despite the agreements of Rambouillet (signed at the time to resolve the conflict with Serbia) and despite the fact that resolution 1244 (on the intervention of the United Nations in Kosovo) included a generic commitment to respect the integrity of the Federal Republic of Yugoslavia, Kosovo's self-determination did not violate any international norm.[2]

Such a broad and flexible recognition of the right of self-determination has been extended as well to the form of its execution. Ideally, a process of secession should be the result of negotiations among the different parties affected by the outcome. In a landmark opinion, Canada's Supreme Court stated that the region of Québec had no unilateral right to dictate the terms of a proposed secession to the other parties to the federation because the Canadian constitution did not recognise the right of self-determination explicitly. However, it immediately added that

> the other provinces and the federal government would have no basis to deny the right of the government of Québec to pursue secession

either. Hence, a Québec vote on the question of secession would have to be followed by negotiations addressing

> the interests of the other provinces, the federal government and Québec and indeed the rights of all Canadians both within and outside Québec, and specifically the rights of minorities.[3]

Still, secession may take place as a result of a unilateral declaration of independence in the case of failed negotiations. In its advisory opinion on Kosovo, the International Court of Justice pointed out that the process of separation was initially conducted in a peaceful and multilateral manner – under the oversight of the international community. In November 2005, the United Nations appointed Finland's former president, Mr Martti Ahtisaari, as a special envoy to Kosovo. In March of 2007, Mr Ahtisaari concluded that

> it is my firm view that the negotiations' potential to produce any mutually agreeable outcome on Kosovo's status is exhausted,

adding that

> that the only viable option for Kosovo is independence, to be supervised for an initial period by the international community

(paragraph 69) and suggesting a procedure, supervised by the international community, towards independence. After neither the UN Security Council nor the Troika, consisting of the United States of America, the European Union and Russia, approved that proposal, the Kosovar representatives voted in favour of secession following fresh elections to the Assembly of Kosovo (paragraph 72). According to the International Court of Justice, that decision 'did not violate general international law, Security Council resolution 1244 (1999) or the Constitutional Framework' or 'any applicable rule of international law' (paragraph 122).

Reasserting the centrality of the right of self-determination as an essential tool to protect human rights and to achieve peace and stability in the international system, the 2014 report of the independent expert on the promotion of a democratic and equitable international order submitted in compliance with the UN Assembly resolution 68/175 emphasised that

> self-determination cannot be understood as a one-time choice, nor does it extinguish with lapse of time because, like the rights to life, freedom and identity, it is too fundamental to be waived

(A/69/272, para. 3) and made all UN state members 'duty bearers' of that right, obligated to 'recognise and promote' it, 'individually and collectively' (ibid., para. 5). The scope of application of the right was expansive since its exercise 'did not end with decolonisation': it extended to 'many indigenous peoples, non self-governing peoples and populations living under occupation' (ibid. para. 72).

Catalonia and the application of the Principle of Self-Determination

If the right of self-determination is not prohibited by international law, under what conditions (beyond those described in the UN Declarations of 1960 and 1970) could its use be justified? The specific conditions that legitimise a process of independence are far from an open-and-shut case. However, most scholars refer back to three principles to justify it: democracy, national self-determination, and secession as a last resort. Although they are not incompatible with each other, they are progressively more demanding in the kinds of conditions or reasons they require to legitimise secession.

The first one, the principle of democracy, has been amply discussed earlier in this chapter. The idea of self-determination was the engine behind the transformation of the international order from the Westphalian system based on states acting as absolute sovereigns within their borders to a system in which individual and collective rights constrain the actions of states with the weak or very imperfect support of international institutions. It is for that reason that, in truly democratic countries, self-determination is seen as a legitimate tool even when it has not been explicitly recognised in their written constitution. As the Supreme Court of Canada stated in its opinion on holding a referendum in Québec, 'the Constitution is not only a written text', but

> encompasses a whole system of principles governing the exercise of constitutional power... federalism, democracy, constitutionalism and the primacy of law, as well as respect for minorities

that should ultimately govern the actions of the states of Canada and their relations with the federation. In light of these principles, the Supreme Court understood that, although there was no 'direct' right of Québec to secession, it was legitimate and constitutional to consult the citizens of that province on that issue. That same interpretation could be applied as well in a liberal, democratic reading of the Spanish Constitution. The latter includes several clauses that enable both the central government or, by delegation, the Catalan government to hold a referendum to determine the support of Catalans toward independence. A positive vote on that question could then be followed by negotiations between the two parties in contention over the terms of the secession, including, if necessary, a reform of the existing constitution. Unfortunately, the Spanish Constitutional Court has taken an extremely restrictive interpretation of the Spanish Constitution – an interpretation that may be in contradiction with the constitutionalised commitment to construe all fundamental rights

> in conformity with the Universal Declaration of Human Rights and international treaties and agreements thereon ratified by Spain (art. 10.2).

According to the principle of national self-determination, a decision to secede should be restricted to a national collectivity, that is, to a body of people that considers itself to have specific national rights. At the end of the day, this seems to be the main point of contention between Spain and Catalonia. The language of the Spanish constitution, negotiated during the democratic transition that followed the death of Franco under the watch of the army and the old Francoist elites, is ambiguous in that regard. Although the constitution refers to the existence of different 'nationalities' in Spain and distinguishes them from 'regions', the Spanish Constitutional Court has denied that the term 'nationality' is identical to 'nation'. Moreover, a majority of Spaniards reject the notion that Catalonia is a nation. However, the Catalan Parliament has repeatedly defined Catalonia as a nation with the support of ample majorities. Most recently, the Catalan Statute of 2006, supported by almost 90 per cent of all Catalan parliamentarians, included the declaration of Catalonia as a nation in its original preamble. In addition, several polls have shown that close to 80 per cent of Catalans favour holding a referendum to determine whether Catalonia should be independent or not. That entails a de facto recognition of Catalonia as a separate national subject that is sovereign to decide its own future.

The right to secede only as a last resort implies that independence may be pursued to put an end to serious and persistent injustices that could not be resolved within the existing political framework. Although there is no full agreement over which situations can be described as serious injustices, they include (ordered from the less to the more contested requirements): (1) human rights violations; (2) unjust military occupations-particularly those that occurred after the explicit prohibition of wars of territorial conquest in 1945; (3) violations, by the central state, of the aspirations of self-government (i.e. the impossibility of reconciling reasonable demands of regional autonomy with the structure of the state) and/or of existing agreements to provide autonomy to a territory (i.e. the systematic encroachment of the central state over regional institutions and policies despite the existing formal agreements); and (4) the fact that a national group is a minority that, permanently outvoted by the majority, has no guarantees that its institutions or any pacts with the majority will be respected.

As we have discussed in preceding chapters, the status of Catalonia has long met conditions (3) and (4). The terms in which the Constitution of 1978 dealt with the Catalan question, and its national status, were too ambiguous. The defence of Catalan culture and language was altogether weak. The specific distribution of powers between the central state and future autonomies remained exceedingly unclear too. Nominally, the Constitution allowed the legislator to confer broad and even exclusive powers over a considerable range of policy domains to regional governments. At the same time, it gave the central government the right to interfere in any matters theoretically devolved to a regional government through the enactment of so-called 'leyes de bases' that could define the whole architecture of any policy area.

The fathers of the Spanish Constitution left the task of resolving all these contradictions – that is, the final power to interpret the exact meaning of the words of the Constitution – in the hands of a paramount political arbitrator, the Constitutional Court. The problem, however, was that the composition of that body remained in the hands of the Spanish majority – here understood as the non-Basque and non-Catalan citizens. As such, it was generally inclined to side against the claims of national minorities. Such a lack of political guarantees became fully apparent during the negotiation and final approval of the reformed Catalan Statute of 2006. The sequential approval of the new autonomy statute by the Catalan Parliament, the Spanish Congress and, finally, via referendum by the Catalan electorate had been arguably introduced as a way to make sure that all parties involved had a say over the level of political decentralisation and that no side could unilaterally change the terms of the agreement. Yet, the Spanish Congress made use of their power to amend that Statute to the point of forcing the Catalan population to choose between an amended legal text that was far removed from the ideal preferences of the consulted citizens and the unsatisfactory status quo that had pushed the Catalan Parliament to write the new autonomy law to start with. More crucially, that procedure, and its alleged protective powers, imploded once the Constitutional Court, overriding the double consent given by the Spanish and the Catalan legislative powers, bestowed upon itself the role of final arbiter of the constitutionality of the Spanish 'State of Autonomies' with its July 2010 ruling. Through this institution, the Spanish national majority made explicit its status as both party and judge in the Spanish political game. The only way to overcome that situation, that is, to guarantee the powers of the Catalan government, would entail reforming the constitution to introduce a mechanism that would give equal institutional weight to both sides – the central and the Catalan governments.

The response of the Spanish institutions before, during and after the 1 October referendum has put Catalonia in the path of fulfilling condition (1), that is, of being the subject of serious human rights abuses. In the last two years, several reports and opinions, coming both from legal experts and international institutions, have denounced the Spanish state for violating fundamental human rights and contravening international norms that actually bind Spain according to the constitution of 1978. Two reports respectively written by international legal observers and by Spanish lawyers, claim that the Spanish state has violated the European Chart of Human Rights on several counts. The decision of the Spanish Constitutional Court to prohibit the Catalan Parliament both from debating the issue of independence and from voting any motion or resolution on that topic in the run-up of the referendum has been seen as a violation of

the fundamental rights to freedom of speech and freedom of association guaranteed by Articles 10 and 11 of the European Convention on Human Rights (ECHR) and Articles 19 and 21 of the International Covenant on Civil and Political Rights (ICCPR) respectively

in a report prepared by, among others, a former President and former Vice President of the European Court of Human Rights. Similarly, the measures taken toward the President of the Catalan Parliament and the arrest of several members of the Catalan administration a few days before the referendum could be seen as infringing articles 5 and 6 of the ECHR.[4] A separate report, signed by 650 Spanish lawyers and published on 26 February 2018, describes and assesses the legality of the actions of the Spanish state that preceded, accompanied and followed the Catalan referendum. Prior to the vote, Spanish authorities allegedly violated the rights to freedom of opinion and expression (ECHR, art. 10 and 11) by gathering information without proper search warrants, suspending several campaign and informative meetings in and outside Catalonia, preventing the broadcasting of public communications by the Catalan party CUP, confiscating material related to the referendum, and closing over 140 websites and dozens of apps. The indiscriminate use of violence by the Spanish police on 1 October, contravened article 3 of the ECHR. Compounding that behaviour and directly contravening ECHR jurisprudence, Spain has not conducted an investigation into those events. Before and after the declaration of independence on 27 October, Spanish courts that do not have the proper jurisdictional powers to oversee those cases charged prominent civil activists and several Catalan ministers with the crimes of rebellion and sedition – without using any police reports as legally required, denying sufficient time to prepare the defence of the detainees, and obviating the fundamental fact that those crimes only happen under conditions of violence that did not take place at any moment in time – and ordered their pre-trial detention without bail. Such behaviour arguably violates the right to an impartial trial (ECHR art 6.1), the principle of legality (ECHR art 7), the right to preparation of defence (art 6.3), among other things. During the electoral campaign that preceded the elections of 21 December 2017, called by the Spanish government after it took over the Catalan government, several candidates were denied their right to participate in electoral meetings or to address voters through normal, direct mass media. After the pro-independence parties won, once again, an absolute majority in Parliament, the Spanish judiciary denied several MPs the right to attend parliamentary sessions (in contradiction with Spain's own constitutional jurisprudence). Finally, the Constitutional Court, which has taken quasi-legislative powers (resulting in a critique from the Venice Commission), blocked the nomination and vote of the leading candidate of the pro-independence majority. All these actions may constitute violations of the right to be elected and to exercise political mandates without interferences (ECHR art. 3) and of the right to not be discriminated (ECHR art. 14).[5]

In an opinion adopted on 26 April 2019, the Working Group on Arbitrary Detentions (WGAD), part of United Nations Human Rights Council, found the Spanish state to be in violation of articles 2, 9 to 11 and 18 to 21 of the Declaration of Human Rights and of articles 2, 14, 19, 21, 22, 25 and 26 of the International Covenant on Civil and Political Rights. The Working Group was responding to a consultation presented by the legal representatives of Joaquim Forn, Josep Rull, Raül Romeva and Dolors Bassa, four Catalan politicians that have been in continuous pre-trial detention since November 2017 in the case of Joaquim Forn and March 2018 in the remaining cases. The WGAD opinion stated that Spanish institutions had violated the right to free speech and free participation as a way to coerce the detainees and to dissuade them from expressing their opinions, participating in politics and seeking the legitimate exercise of the right of self-determination (paragraph 135) and their presumption of innocence (para. 138–142). It also concluded that their prolonged detentions were arbitrary (para. 144) and that the Spanish judicial authorities had violated the existing norms on the distribution of jurisdictional powers (para. 147). The opinion explicitly referred to the decision made by the Supreme Court of Schleswig-Holstein in July of 2018 to deny the extradition of Carles Puigdemont, President of the Catalan government during the independence bid of 2017, requested by Spaniard authorities. Like the German court, the WGAD found the charges of sedition and rebellion made by the Spanish authorities against the Catalan politicians and social leaders in either prison or exile to be groundless. The Catalan independence movement had never engaged in any violence, which constitutes a key prerequisite to establish those charges. Spanish prosecutors, working under the control of the Spanish government, have wrongly stretched the concept of violence to include any peaceful acts that could change the existing constitutional order, thereby jeopardising the entire system of human and political rights.

Internal enlargement: Self-determination within political unions

The case of Catalonia differs from a traditional case of self-determination in a novel and arguably important way. The fact that both Spain and the United Kingdom are member states of the European Union and there is a possibility that Catalonia or Scotland may secede from those states has spurred a growing and interesting debate on their hypothetical standing as independent nations vis-à-vis the EU. London and, particularly, Madrid have suggested that those two territories would be automatically excluded from the EU. Edinburgh and Barcelona have denied this. As pointed out by David Edward, a former judge to the ECJ, the rather stringent conditions that article 50 of the EU Treaties imposes to leave the Union make the Scottish and Catalan position more plausible than the British and Spanish one.

A hardly debated issue, however, is that, independently of the interpretation one may give to article 50, the nature of the European Union suggests quite strongly that the process of Catalan self-determination may be construed as an instance of 'internal enlargement' (as opposed to 'external enlargement' or the entry of new states into the EU). First, the European Union constitutes a supranational organisation that is much closer to the structure of a state than to a standard international organisation. Second, the preamble and initial articles of the Treaties of the European Union insist that the EU was founded on the principles of 'freedom, democracy, equality [and] the rule of law', on the 'respect for human rights, including the rights of persons belonging to minorities', and on the need to have 'decisions taken as closely as possible to the citizen in accordance with the principle of subsidiarity'. That, in turn, puts the EU in the same family of constitutional arrangements of a country like Canada and, therefore, open to the constitutional interpretations of that country's Supreme Court.

It is true that the EU Treaties say little about the intervention of the EU in the political affairs of its members states (with the notable exception of article 7) and contain no provisions regulating a process of internal enlargement, that is, the formation of new states within the Union. Yet, other democratic unions, such as Switzerland and the United States, which did not have any explicit constitutional procedures in that regard, historically engaged in it through rational deliberation and patient negotiations – avoiding, in the process, any costs to the parties involved (included the union or federation itself).

The most recent and geographically closest case involved the secession of the Jura region from the canton of Berne, its constitution as a separate canton, and its reception into the Swiss Confederation 40 years ago to this day. As the Swiss federal authorities emphasised in a report issued at the time of the admission of the canton of Jura into the Confederation, the Swiss constitution of 1874 in place did not contain any mechanism to separate from one canton a part of its population and territory to create a new canton. Indeed, it explicitly guaranteed to all cantons their territory, sovereignty and constitution – in language arguably stronger than the clauses contained in the EU Treaties today.

In the late 1960s, and following a protracted and at times violent conflict between Jura activists and the authorities of the canton of Berne, to which the French-speaking minority of the Jura valley belonged, the Federal Council, the Swiss executive branch, lobbied both the cantonal authorities of Berne and the pro-separation movement in Jura to engage in negotiations while offering itself as a mediator between the two sides. Not much later, in 1968, Berne agreed to establish a 'Comission des bons offices' composed of members appointed by the Federal Council. Following the commission's recommendations, the canton of Berne amended its constitution to recognise the right to self-determination of the Jura. In 1974, 51.9 per cent of the people of Jura approved, in a referendum, to secede from Berne. Three years later, the Swiss confederation accepted the new canton, changing the federal constitution, which enumerates its members, accordingly.

Switzerland, which constitutionalised the procedure of internal enlargement in 1999, is not an exception to cases of internal enlargement. Since independence, the United States has admitted four states that formed part of existing members of the union: Vermont and Kentucky, which split from New York and Virginia respectively, in 1791; Maine, which was part of Massachusetts, in 1820; and West Virginia, which separated from Virginia to remain in the Union, in 1863.

Strengthening and deepening the European Union will not be possible without making it more democratic. A great deal of the political tensions that we are witnessing today in Europe derive from the growing sense that the EU's institutions are far removed from the average European citizen and the EU has become too wedded to the interests of the political elites of its members states. Helping to solve the Catalan question through democratic means may turn out to be a litmus test of the willingness and capacity of the EU to make further progress toward becoming a more perfect, stronger union.

Bibliographical note:

For an introduction to the problem of self-determination in international law, see Falk, R, 'Self-Determination Under International Law: The Coherence of Doctrine Versus the Incoherence of Experience', in Danspeckgruber, W, (ed.), *The Self-Determination of Peoples*, Boulder, 2002.

The ICJ's Advisory Opinion contains a full-fleshed discussion of the question as well:

https://www.webcitation.org/5rRB9e3bz?url=http://www.icj-cij.org/docket/files/141/15987.pdf.

6

The authors

Clara Ponsatí is a Member of European Parliament. She was a Professor of Economics at the School of Economics and Finance at the University of St Andrews and served as Minister of Education in the Catalan Government in 2017.

Antoni Abat Ninet is Professor of Comparative Constitutional Law at the Faculty of Law of the University of Copenhagen and a member of the Centre for European and Comparative Legal Studies.

Enriqueta Aragonès is Research Professor and director at the Institute of Economic Analysis-Institut d'Anàlisi Econòmica (CSIC) and Barcelona Graduate School of Economics affiliated professor.

Carles Boix is the Robert Garrett Professor of Politics and Public Affairs at Princeton University and director of the Institutions and Political Economy Research Group (IPErG) at the University of Barcelona. He is a member of the American Academy of Arts and Sciences.

Albert Carreras is Professor of Economic History at the Department of Economics and Business, Universitat Pompeu Fabra and Barcelona Graduate School of Economics affiliated professor. He served as Deputy Minister of Finances in the Catalan Government.

Xavier Cuadras-Morató is Associate Professor in the Department of Economics and Business at the Universitat Pompeu Fabra (UPF) in Barcelona, Director of the International Business School (ESCI-UPF) and Barcelona Graduate School of Economics affiliated professor.

Jordi Muñoz is Professor of Political Science and fellow at the Institutions and Political Economy Research Group (IPErG) at the University of Barcelona.

Endnotes

Chapter 1

1 https://rm.coe.int/fourth-evaluation-round-corruption-prevention-in-respect-of-members-of/1680779c4d
2 Jean-Paul Costa, Françoise Tulkens, Wolfgang Kaleck and Jessica Simor, 'Catalonian human rights review. Judicial controls in the context of the 1 October referendum'. 19 December 2017.

Chapter 5

1 See Alesina and Spolaore (2005) and Gancia, Ponzetto and Ventura (2017).
2 Comerford and Rodríguez-Mora (2014).

Chapter 6

1 Accordance with International Law of the Unilateral Declaration of Independence in Respect of Kosovo, Advisory Opinion, I.C.J. Reports 2010. Paragraph 79.
2 Advisory Opinion, paragraphs 95 and 114–118.
3 Reference re Secession of Quebec, [1998] 2 SCR 217, 1998 CanLII 793 (SCC).
4 Costa, J. P., F. Tulkens, W. Kalek and J. Simor (2017).
5 Col·lectiu Praga. Report to the Commissioner of Human Rights of the Council of Europe. 26 February 2018. http://collectiupraga.cat/wp-content/uploads/2018/02/Denu%CC%81ncia-CEDH.-26-2-2018-Angle%CC%80s.pdf

Luath Press Limited

committed to publishing well written books worth reading

LUATH PRESS takes its name from Robert Burns, whose little collie Luath (*Gael.*, swift or nimble) tripped up Jean Armour at a wedding and gave him the chance to speak to the woman who was to be his wife and the abiding love of his life. Burns called one of the 'Twa Dogs' Luath after Cuchullin's hunting dog in Ossian's *Fingal*.

Luath Press was established in 1981 in the heart of Burns country, and is now based a few steps up the road from Burns' first lodgings on Edinburgh's Royal Mile. Luath offers you distinctive writing with a hint of unexpected pleasures.

Most bookshops in the UK, the US, Canada, Australia, New Zealand and parts of Europe, either carry our books in stock or can order them for you. To order direct from us, please send a £sterling cheque, postal order, international money order or your credit card details (number, address of cardholder and expiry date) to us at the address below. Please add post and packing as follows: UK – £1.00 per delivery address; overseas surface mail – £2.50 per delivery address; overseas airmail – £3.50 for the first book to each delivery address, plus £1.00 for each additional book by airmail to the same address. If your order is a gift, we will happily enclose your card or message at no extra charge.

Luath Press Limited
543/2 Castlehill
The Royal Mile
Edinburgh EH1 2ND
Scotland
Telephone: +44 (0)131 225 4326 (24 hours)
email: sales@luath. co.uk
Website: www. luath.co.uk